tear repaired 4/85 pg.106

Discard 27

# LANGUAGE FOR DAILY USE

## Phoenix Edition

**Red**

## Curriculum and Instruction

### Dr. Dorothy S. Strickland
Professor of Education
Department of Curriculum and Teaching
Teachers College, Columbia University

### Consulting Educators

Dr. Richard F. Abrahamson, Consultant for Literature
Professor of Education
Department of Curriculum and Instruction
College of Education, University of Houston

Monta J. Akin
Curriculum Coordinator
Leander Independent School District
Leander, Texas

Nola Bacci
Principal
West End Elementary School
Lynbrook, New York

Jennifer Better
Curriculum Coordinator
Cupertino Union School District
Cupertino, California

Betty Gould
Learning Development Specialist
Sachem Central School District
Holbrook, New York

Hildagarde Gray
Librarian
St. John the Baptist School
Pittsburgh, Pennsylvania

Elizabeth Handford
Curriculum Coordinator
Southside Christian School
Greenville, South Carolina

Helen Levy
Librarian
Springfield Elementary School
Princeton City Board of Education
Cincinnati, Ohio

Ozella Nathaniel
Consultant—Elementary Language Arts
Muscogee County Schools
Columbus, Georgia

Rhonda Oster
Second-Grade Teacher
Simi Valley Unified School District
Simi Valley, California

Margaret Rice
Curriculum Coordinator
Leander Independent School District
Leander, Texas

Delia Stafford
Instructional Specialist, K–3
Houston Independent Schools
Houston, Texas

Myrna J. Walters
Consultant/Coordinator of Elementary Reading
and Language Arts
Seminole County Schools
Sanford, Florida

David Zaslow
Writer-in-Residence
South Oregon Public Schools
Ashland, Oregon

*Phoenix Edition*

# LANGUAGE FOR DAILY USE

**Harcourt Brace Jovanovich, Publishers**
**New York   Chicago   San Francisco   Atlanta   Dallas   and   London**

## ACKNOWLEDGMENTS

For permission to reprint copyrighted material, grateful acknowledgment is made to the following sources:

*Atheneum Publishers:* "Zebra" in *Flashlight and Other Poems* by Judith Thurman. Copyright © 1976 by Judith Thurman. (New York: Atheneum, 1976).

*Clarion Books, Ticknor & Fields: A Houghton Mifflin Company, New York:* Adapted from *Little Tuppen* by Paul Galdone. Copyright © 1967 by Paul Galdone.

*Thomas Y. Crowell, Publishers:* Text of "Lots That Animals Do" from *I Often Wish* by Babette Deutsch. Copyright © 1966 by Babette Deutsch. A Funk & Wagnalls Book.

*Doubleday & Company, Inc.: Emma* by Wendy Kesselman, illustrated by Barbara Cooney. Text copyright © 1980 by Wendy Kesselman. Illustrations copyright © 1980 by Barbara Cooney Porter.

*E. P. Dutton, Inc.:* First verse of "At the Library" from *Rhymes About Us* by Marchette Chute. Copyright © 1974 by Marchette Chute.

*Samuel French, Inc.:* First stanza of "Snail" from *More About Me* by John Drinkwater. Copyright 1929.

*Harcourt Brace Jovanovich, Inc.:* Dictionary entries abridged from *The HBJ School Dictionary,* copyright © 1977 by Harcourt Brace Jovanovich, Inc. "Short Sermon" from *Rainbow in the Sky* by Louis Untermeyer, copyright 1935 by Harcourt Brace Jovanovich, Inc.; copyright 1963 by Louis Untermeyer. From "Lines Written for Gene Kelly to Dance To" in *Wind Song,* copyright © 1960 by Carl Sandburg. "A full moon..." by Shiki from *More Cricket Songs: Japanese Haiku,* translated and copyright © 1971 by Harry Behn.

*Harper & Row, Publishers, Inc.:* Text of "First Snow" from *A Pocketful of Poems* by Marie Louise Allen. Copyright © 1957 by Marie Allen Howarth. Dramatization, adapted from the text of "The Mouse and the Winds," from *Mouse Tales* by Arnold Lobel. Copyright © 1972 by Arnold Lobel. *Caution:* "The Mouse and the Winds," from *Mouse Tales* by Arnold Lobel is the sole property of the author and is fully protected by copyright. This adaptation may not be acted by professionals or amateurs without formal permission of the publisher. All inquiries should be addressed to Harper & Row, Publishers, Inc., 10 East 53rd Street, New York, New York 10022.

*Highlights for Children, Inc., Columbus, Ohio:* "Jumbo King of the Circus" by D. A. Woodliff. Copyright © 1980, Highlights for Children, Inc.

*The Instructor Publications, Inc.:* "World of Sound" by Jane Krows from *Teacher,* May 1961. Copyright © by Macmillan Professional Magazines.

*Alfred A. Knopf, Inc.:* "Poem" by Langston Hughes. Copyright 1932 and renewed 1960 by Langston Hughes. "Winter Moon" by Langston Hughes. Copyright 1926 by Alfred A. Knopf, Inc., and renewed 1954 by Langston Hughes. Both poems are taken from *The Dream Keeper and Other Poems* by Langston Hughes.

*Ruth Krauss, 24 Owenoke, Westport, Conn. 06880:* "Snow Melting" by Ruth Krauss in *The Cantilever Rainbow.*

*The Lois Lenski Covey Foundation, Inc.:* From "Library" from *City Poems* by Lois Lenski. Copyright © 1971 by Lois Lenski.

*Macmillan Publishing Co., Inc.:* "The Moon's the North Wind's Cooky" from *Collected Poems* by Vachel Lindsay. Copyright 1914 by Macmillan Publishing Co., Inc., renewed 1942 by Elizabeth C. Lindsay. "Who Has Seen the Wind?" from *Sing-Song* by Christina Rossetti.

*G. P. Putnam's Sons:* "Snow" and "Brooms" from *Everything & Anything* by Dorothy Aldis. Copyright 1925, 1926, 1927; renewed © 1953, 1954, 1955 by Dorothy Aldis.

*Marian Reiner for Myra Cohn Livingston:* Stanzas from "Rain," and "Feet" from *Whispers and Other Poems* by Myra Cohn Livingston. Copyright © 1958 by Myra Cohn Livingston.

*Western Publishing Company, Inc.:* "Kite Days" by Mark Sawyer from *Story Parade.* Copyright 1939, renewed 1967 by Story Parade, Inc.

PRINTED IN THE UNITED STATES OF AMERICA

ISBN 0–15–317003–4

## PHOTO CREDITS

## ART CREDITS

# CONTENTS

**UNIT 5** 119

# LANGUAGE
Listening
and Speaking

# STUDY SKILLS
Learning About
ABC Order

# COMPOSITION
Writing Rhymes

# LITERATURE
Reading Poetry

Look at the pictures. Which people are listening? Which people are speaking? Choose a picture to talk about. Then listen as your friends tell about different pictures.

You hear and say many things each day. What do you listen to each day? Tell three things you heard in school today. Did any of your classmates hear the same things?

Which do you think you do more often, listen or speak? Think about it. Which people did you speak with today?

# LANGUAGE

## *Lesson 1: Listening Politely*

Look at the picture. The children are listening to the teacher, Mr. Santos. They want to find out something. What is it?

### *Think and Discuss*

You can learn about things in many ways. You can look. You can listen. Here are some rules to help you.

> **How to Listen Politely**
>
> 1. **Look at the speaker.**
> 2. **Pay attention to what the speaker says.**
> 3. **Think about what you hear.**

Think of other listening rules. How should you sit when you listen? Should you talk? Suppose you do not understand something. What should you do?

## Practice

**A.** One word is missing from each listening rule. Read the three words. Write the correct word for each sentence.

talking      questions     Sit

**1.** _____ up straight.
**2.** Don't talk when others are _____.
**3.** Politely ask _____ if you do not understand something.

## Apply

**B. 4.** Make a chart about good listening with your class. First talk about the rules. Then write them on the chart.

## HOW OUR LANGUAGE GROWS

Many of the words we use today are very old. The way we say some words has changed. The way we spell some words has also changed.

Look at each word below. Each word is spelled as it was long ago. Write it the way it is spelled today. Check the spelling in the box.

man
dog
yard
cat
girl
baby

**1.** dogge    **2.** girle    **3.** mann
**4.** catte    **5.** babie    **6.** yarde

# Lesson 2: Speaking in Class

The children in Ms. Drake's class are taking turns speaking. It is Janet's turn.

## Think and Discuss

Everyone is listening politely to Janet. They are following the listening rules they learned. There are speaking rules too. Here are some of them.

> **How to Speak in Class**
>
> 1. **Stand up straight.**
> 2. **Say your words clearly.**
> 3. **Speak so that everyone can hear you.**

Think of other speaking rules. What should you do before you begin? Where should you look?

## Practice

**A.** One word is missing from each speaking rule. Read the two words. Write the correct word for each sentence.

      everyone      Think

**1.** _____ about what you want to say.
**2.** Speak so that _____ can hear you.

## Apply

**B. 3.** Talk about the rules for good speaking with your class. Then write them on a chart.

# Lesson 3: Listening to Directions

Martin is telling Nora directions to his house. Why must she listen carefully to him?

## Think and Discuss

Read the rules for listening to directions. Tell why each rule is important.

> **How to Listen to Directions**
>
> 1. **Listen carefully.**
> 2. **Picture each direction.**
> 3. **Say the directions to yourself.**
> 4. **If you do not understand something, ask questions.**

## Practice

**A.** Listen as your teacher reads the directions. Trace a path on the map with your finger.

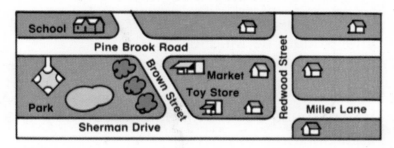

## Apply

**B.** Play <u>Follow the Directions</u>. Your teacher will tell you the rules.

# Lesson 4: Talking on the Telephone

Read this telephone conversation.

> **Mary:** Hello.
> **Mr. Hall:** Hello, Mary. Is your dad at home?
> **Mary:** Who is calling please?
> **Mr. Hall:** It's Mr. Hall.
> **Mary:** Just a minute please, Mr. Hall. I will call my father.

## Think and Discuss

You speak and listen when you use the telephone. What did Mary say when she answered? What did Mr. Hall say first? How was Mary polite?

## Practice

**A. 1.** Practice the telephone conversation with a partner. One person should be Mary. The other should be Mr. Hall.

## Apply

**B.** Act out these calls. One person can call. The other person can answer.

**2.** Your friend asks you to come to a party.

**3.** Your aunt asks to speak to your mother.

**4.** Someone asks if this is the fish store.

# Lesson 5: Making Introductions

## Think and Discuss

These rules tell how to introduce people.
Why is each a good rule to follow?

> **How to Introduce People**
>
> 1. **Sometimes you introduce a young person to an older person. When you do, say the older person's name first.**
> 2. **Say the names clearly.**
> 3. **Tell something about the person you are introducing.**

## Practice

**A.** Act out these introductions.

1. Introduce a friend to your father.
2. Introduce a new student to the teacher.

## Apply

**B. 3.** Have two friends pretend to be storybook people. Introduce them to each other.

# LANGUAGE REVIEW

## Listening Rules    pages 2–3

Which three rules tell about listening? Write them.

1. Look at your feet.
2. Look at the speaker.
3. Pay attention.
4. Think about what you hear.
5. Say your words clearly.

## Speaking Rules    page 4

Which three rules tell about speaking correctly in class? Write them.

6. Do not ask questions.
7. Stand up straight.
8. Say your words clearly.
9. Pay attention.
10. Speak loudly.

## Directions    page 5

Which four rules tell about following directions? Write them.

11. Listen carefully.
12. Picture what you should do.
13. Look out the window.
14. Say the directions to yourself.
15. Ask questions if you do not understand something.

## Telephone Calls page 6

Which four rules are about using the telephone?
Write them.

16. Say "Hello" politely when you answer the telephone.
17. Think about something else.
18. Listen to find out who is calling.
19. Say the older person's name first when you introduce two people.
20. Do not talk too long.
21. Write down telephone messages for other people.

## Introductions page 7

Which three rules tell how to introduce people?
Write them.

22. Say the words to yourself.
23. When you introduce a young person to an older person, say the older person's name first.
24. Say both names clearly.
25. Tell something about the person you are introducing.

## Applying Listening and Speaking

26. Tell a friend directions to someplace. Follow the speaking rules on your class chart. Listen to any questions your friend asks. Answer the questions. Be polite.

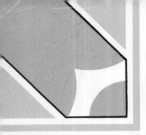

# STUDY SKILLS

## *Lesson 6: Understanding ABC Order*

Point to each letter below as you say it.

abcdefghijklmnopqrstuvwxyz

## **Think and Discuss**

The order of letters from A to Z is called **ABC order.** ABC order never changes.

Sometimes we put words in ABC order too. Look at the first letters of these words.

1. apple    2. balloon    3. candle

The first letters were used to put the words in ABC order. Add some more words to the list in ABC order.

## **Practice**

**A.** Think of the missing letters. Write each group of letters. Put in the missing ones.

**1.** A, ____, ____, D, E    **2.** g, h, ____, ____, k
**3.** ____, L, M, ____, O    **4.** ____, t, ____, v, w

**B.** These lists are not in ABC order. Write them in ABC order.

| | |
|---|---|
| **5. Things to Make**<br> hats<br> games<br> food | **6. Things for Games**<br> prizes<br> markers<br> balloons |

## *Apply*

**C. 7.–12.** Pretend that you played a word game at a party. Write six words that begin with the letters shown. Put the words in ABC order.

k    o    n    m    l    p

## *A Challenge*

These words are in a code. Each letter stands for the letter before it in ABC order. Find out what the message means. Then write a new message.

ibqqz    cjsuiebz    up    zpv!

| | |
|---|---|
| Code: | b c d e f g h i j k l m n o p q r s t u v w x y z a |
| Alphabet: | A B C D E F G H I J K L M N O P Q R S T U V W X Y Z |

# Lesson 7: Listing Words in ABC Order

Eli is going to the store. Read the list he made. Eli wrote the list in a special way.

apples
bananas
cheese

## Think and Discuss

Did Eli use ABC order to write his list? Look at the first letter of each word. Why does the word <u>apples</u> come before <u>bananas</u>? Why does <u>bananas</u> come before <u>cheese</u>?

Now look at this list. The words are in ABC order.

bananas
beans
bread

The first letter of each word is the same. Look at the second letter of each word. The second letters were used to put the words in ABC order.

Are the groups of words below in ABC order?

| | |
|---|---|
| tea<br>tomato<br>tuna | salt<br>soap<br>stew |

## Practice

**A.** Are these lists in ABC order? Write <u>yes</u> or <u>no</u>.

1. cabbage, lettuce, radishes
2. milk, lemonade, juice
3. butter, cereal, crackers
4. ham, honey, jelly
5. bananas, bran, eggs
6. liver, lamb, mutton
7. noodles, nuts, rice
8. yams, yeast, yogurt
9. oil, oats, oranges
10. peas, popcorn, pickles

**B.** Write each list in ABC order.

11. celery, carrots, cucumbers
12. plums, prunes, peaches
13. flour, fruit, fish
14. peas, corn, cream
15. meat, limes, lemons

## Apply

**C. 16.–20.** Think of two words that begin with **m.**
Then think of three words that begin with **n.**
Write the five words in ABC order.

# COMPOSITION

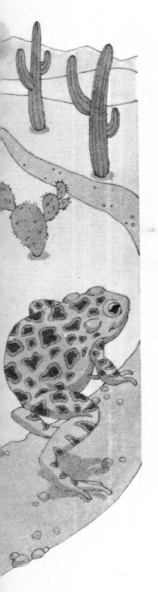

## *Lesson 8: Writing Rhymes*

Ann and Nan like to make up rhymes. Read their rhymes.

Did you ever wish
To be a little fish?

Did you ever wonder
What is as loud as thunder?

### *Think and Discuss*

Rhyming words end with the same sounds. Read the two rhymes above. Name the rhyming words.

Think of a rhyming word to end this rhyme.

A little spotted toad
Hopped beside me on the _____.

### *Practice*

**A. 1.–5.** Listen as your teacher reads some directions.

**B.** Find the word to end each rhyme. Write it.

**6.** Leave my dog alone
   When it has a _____.

   flea
   bone

**7.** Our horse runs fast,
   It will not be _____.

   first
   last

**C.** Use the correct word to end each rhyme.

rest    sleep

**8.** The bird sits on its nest,
And takes a little _____.

**9.** Tell me, little sheep,
When will you go to _____?

## *Apply*

**D. 10.** Here are some rhyming words. Choose
one pair of words. Write a rhyme.

get, pet      take, lake
pick, stick   need, seed
cook, book    heard, word

**To Memorize**

Lots that animals can do
I often wish that I could, too.
But when I think some more, I see
It's much better to be
        ME.

Babette Deutsch

What can an animal do that you cannot do?
What can you do that an animal cannot do?

# Lesson 9: Using Rhyme in Poetry

Listen as your teacher reads this poem.

### The Robin

Little Robin Redbreast
Sat upon a tree,
He sang merrily,
As merrily as could be.

He nodded with his head,
And his tail waggled he,
As little Robin Redbreast
Sat upon a tree.

## Think and Discuss

"The Robin" has four lines in the first part.
It also has four lines in the second part.

Look at the first part of the poem. Which words rhyme with <u>tree</u>?

Now look at the second part of the poem. Which word rhymes with <u>he</u>? Name some other words that rhyme with <u>he</u>.

## Practice

**A. 1.** Finish the rhymes in this poem. Write a word for each blank. Use the words <u>giraffe</u>, <u>bear</u>, <u>whale</u>, and <u>bee</u>.

### Animal Manners

Please don't laugh
When you meet a _____.
Bend down on one knee
To shake hands with a _____.
Bring your own chair
If you dine with a _____.
Don't read your mail
In front of a _____.

**B. 2.** Finish this poem. Make line 1 rhyme with line 2. Make line 3 rhyme with line 4. Use the words <u>best</u>, <u>song</u>, <u>long</u>, and <u>nest</u>.

The baby birds eat all day _____.
They do not fly or sing a _____.
Worms are the food that they like _____,
Parents bring worms to the _____.

## Apply

**C. 3.** Find a poem you like. Choose one that has rhyme. Read the poem out loud. Ask your classmates to name the rhyming words.

# LITERATURE

## Lesson 10: Reading Poetry

Read the poem. Listen for words that rhyme.

### Kite Days

A kite, a sky, and a good firm breeze,
And acres of ground away from trees,
And one hundred yards
   of clean, strong string —
O boy, O boy! I call that Spring!

Mark Sawyer

### Think and Discuss

Read the next poem. How is it like the poem
at the top of the page? How is it different?

Spring is when the grass turns green and
   glad.
Spring is when the new grass comes up
   and says, "Hey, hey! Hey, hey!"
Be dizzy now and turn your head upside down
   and see how the world looks upside down.
Be dizzy now and turn a cartwheel, and see
   the good earth through a cartwheel.

Carl Sandburg

Read these poems about the moon.

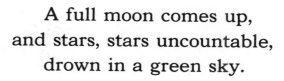

## Winter Moon

How thin and sharp is the moon tonight!
How thin and sharp and ghostly white
Is the slim curved crook of the moon tonight!

Langston Hughes

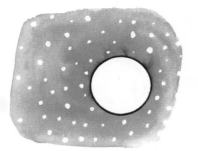

A full moon comes up,
and stars, stars uncountable,
drown in a green sky.

Shiki

## The Moon's the North Wind's Cooky

The Moon's the North Wind's cooky,
He bites it day by day,
Until there's but a rim of scraps
That crumble all away.

The South Wind is a baker.
He kneads clouds in his den,
And bakes a crisp new moon that . . . greedy
North . . . Wind . . . eats . . . again!

Vachel Lindsay

Which of these poems rhyme? What does the moon look like in each poem? These poets painted three different pictures of the moon.

## *Practice*

**A.** Listen as your teacher reads these poems.

**1.** Which poem has rhyming words? Name the words.

**2.** Which poem does not have rhyming words?

**World of Sound**

I went to the city and what did I hear?
The traffic drone
The telephone
The workman's crane
The subway train
The policeman's tweet
The taxi's beep.

I went to the country and what did I hear?
The redbird's call
The waterfall
The young calf's bawl
The soft rainfall
The buzzing bee
And wind in the tree.

Wherever you live in country or town
You always dwell in a world of sound.

Jane W. Krows

### Zebra

white sun
black
fire escape,

morning
grazing like a zebra
outside my window.

Judith Thurman

## *Apply*

**B. 3.** Find a poem you like. Practice reading it
out loud. Read it for the class.

---

## A BOOK TO READ

Title: **There Are Rocks in My Socks!**
**Said the Ox to the Fox.**
Author: Patricia Thomas
Publisher: Lothrop, Lee & Shepard

Poor ox! He tried to take the rocks from his socks.
He got:
A tack in his back, and a rail on his tail.
T-h-e-n a bee on his knee, followed by —
A whack on the nose! (How do you suppose?)

Poor ox. A smart old bird saved the day.

# 1 UNIT TEST

- **Listening and Speaking Rules**   pages 2–4

  Write <u>Listening Rules</u> on your paper. Copy the three rules about listening. Then write <u>Speaking Rules</u> on your paper. Copy the three speaking rules.

  1. Think about what you want to say.
  2. Look at the speaker.
  3. Pay attention.
  4. Say your words clearly.
  5. Think about what you hear.
  6. Speak so that everyone can hear you.

- **Telephone Conversations and Introductions**   pages 6–7

  Read each sentence. Write the letter for the correct way to speak to others.

  7. **a.** Who is this? Give me Dan.
     **b.** Hello. May I speak to Dan please?

  8. **a.** Mother, this is Suki, a classmate.
     **b.** Mother, here is Suki.

- **ABC Order**   pages 10–11

  Write the missing letters for ABC order.

  1. v, w, _____, _____, z
  2. B, C, _____, E, _____
  3. _____, r, _____, t, u
  4. l, _____, _____, o, p

## Words in ABC Order   pages 12–13

Write the letter for each group of words that is in ABC order.

**5. a.** came, doctor, dug
   **b.** came, dug, doctor

**6. a.** nut, note, picture
   **b.** note, nut, picture

## Writing Rhymes   pages 14–15

Choose the word in ( ) that finishes each rhyme. Write it.

**1.** Two dogs had a fight,
   It went on all _____.   (around, night)

**2.** I need some money,
   To buy bread and _____.   (toys, honey)

## Reading Poetry   pages 18–21

Read the poem. Find a rhyming word for each underlined word. Write the rhyming words.

### Way Down South Where Bananas Grow

Way down South where bananas grow,
A grasshopper stepped on an elephant's toe.
The elephant said, with tears in his eyes,
"Pick on somebody your own size!"

Anonymous

**2**

# LANGUAGE
Learning About Sentences

## STUDY SKILLS
Reporting Information

# COMPOSITION
Writing Sentences

## LITERATURE
Reading a Story

Words are put together to make sentences. Sentences often tell something. Sometimes sentences ask something.

Choose one of the pictures. Make up a sentence that tells something about it. What might one person in the picture be asking? Say it in a sentence.

In one picture a girl is writing sentences. Many sentences together can tell a story. Can you tell a story about one of the pictures? Use asking and telling sentences.

# LANGUAGE

## Lesson 1: Understanding Sentences

Look at the pictures. Read the words.

1. Rosa swings from the tree.
2. Mai hides behind the leaves.

### Think and Discuss

The groups of words above make two **sentences.** A sentence is a group of words that tells a complete thought. Every sentence begins with a capital letter.

Who is named in each sentence? What does sentence 1 tell about Rosa? What does sentence 2 tell about Mai? Now read this group of words.

3. climbs higher and higher

This group of words does not tell a complete thought. It does not begin with a capital letter. Is it a sentence?

## Practice

**A.** Look at each group of words. Write <u>yes</u> if the words make a sentence. Write <u>no</u> if they do not.

1. a bird
2. Leaves fall off trees.
3. oranges and lemons
4. Roots grow into the ground.
5. on the tree trunk
6. can climb very well
7. The tree has branches.
8. in the spring

**B.** Write these sentences correctly.

9. the boy likes to climb trees.
10. birds build nests in trees.
11. this boat is made from a log.
12. a tree grows from a seed.
13. leaves grow on tree branches.

## Apply

**C.** Now write two sentences of your own. Use the words below in your sentences.

14. A bird _____.
15. _____ ran up a tree.

# Lesson 2: Understanding Parts of a Sentence

Look at the picture and the sentence parts.

1. _____ rolled quickly.    2. A wheel _____.

## Think and Discuss

What rolled out of the wagon? Add words to make a sentence. What happened to a wheel? Add words to make a sentence.

## Practice

**A.** Read the words in the box. Use the words to complete each sentence. Write each sentence.

| have four wheels |
| Many toys |
| The wagon |
| pulls the wagon |

1. _____ are in the wagon.
2. _____ is red.
3. Wagons _____.
4. The boy _____.

## Apply

**B. 5.–6.** Think of two things you can put in a wagon. What might happen? Write a sentence about each.

# Lesson 3: Understanding Statements

Look at the picture. Read these sentences.

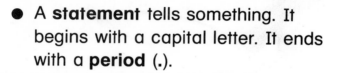

1. Sam Bluehouse tells stories to children.
2. The children like to listen to him.

## Think and Discuss

Sentences 1 and 2 are telling sentences. A telling sentence is called a **statement.** Sentence 1 tells what Sam does. What does sentence 2 tell? Notice the mark at the end of the sentences.

> ● A **statement** tells something. It begins with a capital letter. It ends with a **period** (.).

## Practice

**A.** Copy each statement that is written correctly.

1. Sam Bluehouse is a chief.
2. the children listen
3. His mother told Sam the stories.

**B.** Write this statement correctly.

4. the stories are very old

## Apply

**C. 5.–6.** Write two statements. Tell something about Sam Bluehouse. Tell something about the children.

# Lesson 4: Understanding Questions

Look at the picture. Then read the two sentences.

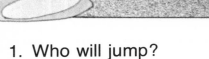

1. Who will jump?    2. Is the dog barking?

*yes*

## Think and Discuss

Sentences 1 and 2 ask something. What does each sentence ask? Notice the mark at the end of the sentences.

> ● A **question** asks something. It begins with a capital letter. It ends with a **question mark** (**?**).

## Practice

**A.** Copy only the sentences that ask questions.

1. Rain makes puddles.       2. Where is the sun?
3. Do you like rain?          4. We are all wet.
5. Are you coming too?        6. Is this my hat?

**B.** Write each question correctly.

7. will it rain today
8. where are my boots
9. did you hear that thunder

## *Apply*

**C. 10.–12.** Pretend it is a sunny day. Write three questions. Use the word <u>sun</u> in each of your sentences.

# HOW OUR LANGUAGE GROWS

People who cannot hear or speak use sign language. Sometimes they use a hand or a body sign for a whole word. At other times hand signs <u>spell</u> words.

See how well you can read and spell sign language. Spell these words to a friend. Use sign language.

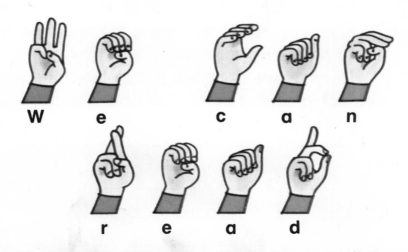

W     e         c     a     n

r     e     a     d

# Lesson 5: Understanding Word Order

Dinah's mother left her a note.

> Dear Dinah,
>     shopping going I am.
> back be will four o'clock at I.
> This note is a puzzle.
>                         Mom

## Think and Discuss

A good sentence has its words in correct order. The word order gives the sentence meaning.

Which groups of words in Mom's note are not sentences? Why not? Which group of words is a sentence? Put all the words in the correct order. Read Mom's note correctly.

Dinah wrote a note to her mother. The words are not in correct order. Tell what the note should say.

> Dear Mom,
>     back noon I be at will.
>                         Dinah

## Practice

**A.** Read each group of words below. Write the ones that are in correct order.

1. Mother wrote a note to Dinah.
2. the table Was on the note?
3. the note laughed Dinah at.
4. Mother will be home soon.
5. She went shopping.

**B.** Put the words in correct order. Write each sentence correctly.

6. came Mother home.
7. she Guess saw what?
8. saw note a She.
9. it wrote Dinah.
10. of order some words out Were?

## Apply

**C. 11.–12.** Write two sentences with the words in the correct order. Then write the sentences again. Mix up the order of the words in each sentence. Give your sentences to a classmate. Ask your classmate to write the sentences correctly. Then check your work together.

# Lesson 6: Using <u>I</u> in Sentences

Read the two sentences. Notice the underlined words.

1. <u>I</u> sing songs with my sister.
2. <u>Ingrid</u> <u>and</u> <u>I</u> sing songs.

## Think and Discuss

Find the word <u>I</u> in sentence 1. How is the word <u>I</u> written?

Read sentence 2. Who sing songs? Notice that <u>I</u> comes after the name of another person.

> ● When you speak of another person and yourself, always name yourself last. The word <u>I</u> is always written with a capital letter.

## Practice

**A.** Copy the groups of words that are written correctly.

1. hazel and i      Hazel and I
2. Eric and I       i and eric

**B.** Choose the correct words in ( ). Then write each sentence.

3. (Lee and I, I and Lee) learned a song.
4. Then (Lee and i, Lee and I) sang it.
5. Soon (I and Tod, Tod and I) heard a noise.
6. (I and Jan, Jan and I) laughed at the dog.

## *Apply*

**C. 7.–8.** Write two sentences about a friend and yourself. Tell something your friend and you did. Use the word <u>I</u> correctly.

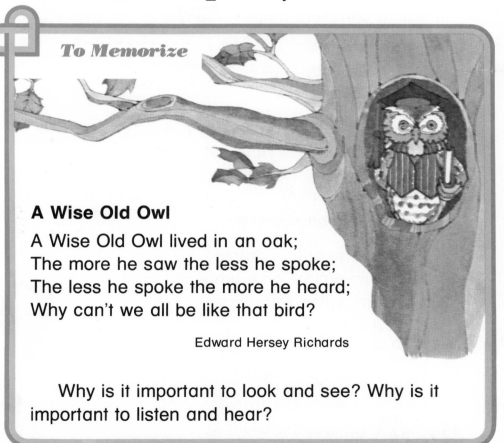

*To Memorize*

**A Wise Old Owl**

A Wise Old Owl lived in an oak;
The more he saw the less he spoke;
The less he spoke the more he heard;
Why can't we all be like that bird?

Edward Hersey Richards

Why is it important to look and see? Why is it important to listen and hear?

# LANGUAGE REVIEW

## Sentences    pages 26–27

Write <u>yes</u> if the words make a sentence. Write <u>no</u> if they do not make a sentence.

1. The class made drums.
2. tin cans
3. played a song
4. Jo sang for us.

## Parts of a Sentence    page 28

Read the sentences below the box. Write words from the box to complete each sentence.

| The drum    ran after it |
|---|

5. _____ rolled on the floor.
6. Tom _____ .

## Statements    page 29

Write each sentence correctly.

7. tin cans make fine drums
8. some have cloth on each end
9. the cloth is tied with yarn

## Questions    pages 30–31

Write each asking sentence correctly.

10. which cloth should I use
11. may I make a big drum

## Statements and Questions    pages 29–31

If a sentence is a statement, write <u>statement</u>. If it is a question, write <u>question</u>.

12. I will make a round drum.
13. Is it hard to make a drum?
14. Do we need help?
15. The teacher will answer our questions.
16. I will work with Julie.

## Word Order in Sentences    pages 32–33

Write the words in correct sentence order.

17. fixed his drum Adam.
18. the Will join he parade?
19. begin the parade will When?

## Using I    pages 34–35

Choose the correct word in (   ). Then write each sentence.

20. Julie and (I, i) worked together.
21. First Julie and (i, I) covered a can.
22. Then Julie and (I, i) tied the ends.
23. Tomorrow Julie and (i, I) will finish.

## Applying Questions and Statements

24.–25. Pretend you are going to make a drum. Write one question that you might ask yourself. Then write one statement about the drum.

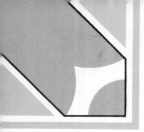

# STUDY SKILLS

## *Lesson 7: Recognizing True and False Statements*

Read these sentences. Which can really happen?

1. Fish live in water.    2. Fish can write.

### *Think and Discuss*

Sentence 1 is a **true** statement. You know fish live in water. Sentence 2 is not true. It is a **false** statement. Can fish write in real life?

### *Practice*

**A.** Write the true statements.

1. Fish can swim.
2. Fish bark at cars.
3. Fish have fur.
4. People catch fish.
5. Fish walk and run.
6. Fish have fins.

### *Apply*

**B. 7.–10.** Write two true statements about boats. Then write two false statements about boats.

### *A Challenge*

Find out if each sentence is true or false.

1. Otters like to play.    2. Baby otters cannot see.

# Lesson 8: Completing Forms

People often are asked to fill out forms. Study this form for a library card.

Hillcrest School Library

Name _Dwayne  Jackson_____

Address _71. Heather Drive_____

_____ Flint, Michigan  48212_____

School _Cresmont_____

Grade _Second_____

## Think and Discuss

What information did Dwayne write on the form? Notice that only one word is given on each line. The word tells what to write. Did Dwayne fill out the form correctly?

## Practice

**A.** Make up another form for a library card. Pretend you are asked to fill it out. Write your information neatly on each line.

## Apply

**B.** Work with your class. Make up a form for a pet show. Write a word on each line. Draw a line where you can write the information.

# COMPOSITION

## *Lesson 9: Writing Statements and Questions*

Karen wrote some sentences about the zoo. Read her sentences.

1. Have you ever seen a seal?
2. We saw the seals at the zoo.

Which sentence is a statement? Which sentence asks a question?

## *Think and Discuss*

Karen's sentences begin with capital letters. They end with special marks. What mark goes at the end of a statement? What mark goes at the end of a question?

Be careful when you write sentences. Be sure to begin and end each sentence correctly.

## Practice

**A.** Study the sentences below. Then close your book. Take out a piece of paper. Write the sentences as your teacher reads them. Remember to begin and end your sentences correctly.

1. The zookeeper is walking.
2. He carries a pail.
3. What is inside the pail?
4. Do seals like fish?

**B.** Write these statements correctly.

5. the people feed the seals
6. the seals clap and bark

**C.** Write these questions correctly.

7. do you see the big seal
8. is that seal jumping for the fish

## Apply

**D. 9.–10.** Study the picture below. Then write two statements that tell something about the picture.

# Lesson 10: Editing Sentences

Some children watched a puppet show. Tamara wrote about the show. Read what she wrote.

1. we watched a puppet show.
2. i liked the red puppet ⊙

## Think and Discuss

Tamara made some mistakes in her sentences. She used special marks to correct her mistakes. The marks Tamara used are called **editing marks.**

Tamara used this mark ≡ to make a capital letter. Why did she add those capital letters?

Tamara used this mark ⊙ to make a period. Where did she add a period? Why did she need one there?

Now Tamara can copy her sentences correctly. Her sentences will be clearer and easier to read.

## Practice

**A.** Write Tamara's sentences correctly. You will write two sentences. Show the changes Tamara made.

## Apply

**B.** Look at the sentences you wrote in Lesson 9. Did you begin each sentence with a capital letter? Did you end each sentence with the correct mark? Use editing marks to show changes. Then copy your sentences correctly.

## MECHANICS PRACTICE

### Writing Sentences

- Every sentence begins with a capital letter.
- Use a period (.) at the end of a statement.
- Use a question mark (?) at the end of a question.
- Always write the word I with a capital letter.

Write these sentences correctly. Use capital letters, periods, and question marks where they belong.

1. the sun was behind a cloud
2. the sky turned gray
3. i felt a cold wind
4. jim and i were at the lake
5. was it going to snow
6. why did the weather change

# LITERATURE

### Lesson 11: Reading a Story

Read along as your teacher reads the story aloud.

## Emma

by Wendy Kesselman

It was Emma's birthday. She was seventy-two years old.

Emma had four children, seven grandchildren, and fourteen great-grandchildren. Emma was happy when her family came to visit. She baked noodle puddings and chocolate cream pies. She put flowers everywhere.

Her family brought her lots of presents, but they never stayed very long. So most of the time Emma was all alone. Sometimes she was very lonely.

The only company she had was her orange cat, Pumpkinseed. They sat together outside and curled their toes in the sun. They listened to the woodpecker tapping at the old apple tree. Sometimes Pumpkinseed got stuck at the top of the tree, and Emma had to climb up and rescue him. Emma didn't mind. She loved climbing trees.

She loved all kinds of simple things. She loved to see the snow come right up to her doorstep. She loved to sit and dream about the little village across the mountains where she grew up. When Emma told her family about the things she loved, they laughed and said to each other, "Poor Emma. She must be getting old."

For her seventy-second birthday the family gave Emma a painting of her little village across the mountains. Emma hung the painting on the wall. "It's beautiful," she said to them. To herself she thought, "That's not how I remember my village at all." Every day Emma looked at the painting and frowned. Every day her frown grew a little deeper.

One day she made up her mind. She went to the store and bought paints and brushes and an easel. Then Emma sat by the window and painted her village just the way she remembered it. When she finished she took the other painting off the wall and hung hers up instead. Every day Emma looked at her painting and smiled.

When her family came to visit, Emma put the other painting back again. As soon as they left she switched it for her own. Then one day Emma forgot. When the family was in the middle of dinner, one of Emma's grandchildren pointed to the wall. "Where did that painting come from? It's not the one we gave you!"

Emma looked up. Emma looked down. Everyone kept right on looking at the painting, and they all kept asking, "Yes, where did it come from?"

Finally Emma said, "Me," very softly. "I did it."

"You!" they all cried out together.

Emma hurried to hide the painting in the closet. "Stop!" cried her family. "Don't hide it away! It's beautiful! Why don't you paint another one?"

"I have," said Emma.

She brought twenty more paintings out of the closet. From that day Emma kept painting and she never stopped. She painted hundreds of paintings. Her paintings covered the walls. They filled the closets. They hung in the kitchen cupboards. Emma was surrounded by the friends and places she loved. She was never lonely again.

## Think and Discuss

Most sentences in a story are about one thing. That thing is called the main idea. What is the main idea in <u>Emma</u>?

The sentences in a story are often in an order. They tell what happened first, next, and last. How does Emma feel at the beginning of the story?

## Practice

**A.** Write three sentences about <u>Emma</u> on a piece of paper. Tell what happened in the beginning, the middle, and the end of the story.

## Apply

**B.** Draw a picture on a piece of paper. Show the main idea of the story. Write a sentence that tells the main idea.

## A BOOK TO READ

Title: **The Little Painter**
Authors: Ralph and Jill Marchant
Publisher: Carolrhoda Books

Whenever the little painter painted a house, it was a mess! Then one day he met a strange old man. The man sold him a small can of magic paint. Read the story to find out what happened next.

# 2 UNIT TEST

● **Sentences**   pages 26–27

**1.** Write the letter of the word group that is a sentence.

**a.** many bees    **b.** the flowers
**c.** Honey tastes good.    **d.** can sting

● **Capital Letters and Punctuation Marks**   pages 26–31

Write each sentence correctly. Use capital letters. Use a period or a question mark.

**2.** do you like bees    **3.** why are bees so busy
**4.** they make honey    **5.** honey is sweet

● **Statements and Questions**   pages 29–31

Read each sentence. If the sentence is a statement, write <u>statement</u>. If the sentence is a question, write <u>question</u>.

**6.** Bees are yellow and black.    **7.** What is a queen bee?
**8.** How many legs do bees have?    **9.** A bee sting hurts for a short time.

● **Word Order**   pages 32–33

Put the words in correct order. Write each sentence correctly.

**10.** land Bees on flowers.    **11.** hives Do in live bees?

## Using I

Write the sentence correctly.

**12.** During the picnic Barb and i saw a bee.

## True and False Statements
page 38

Write <u>true</u> or <u>false</u> for each sentence.

**1.** Bees wear clothes.     **2.** Bees can fly.

## Completing Forms
page 39

**3.** Pretend you are getting a dog tag for your dog. Make up a form to fill out. Leave space for a name, address, and telephone number. Leave space for the dog's name too. Then fill in the information correctly.

## Writing Statements and Questions
pages 40–41

**1.–2.** Write a question about a bee and a flower. Write a statement to answer the question.

## Editing Sentences
pages 42–43

**3.** Read the sentences you just wrote. Make sure everything is correct. Improve your sentences if you can.

## Reading Stories
pages 44–47

**1.–2.** Read a story in one of your books. Tell what happens at the beginning of the story. Tell the main idea of the story.

# MAINTENANCE and REVIEW

**Directions**    page 5

Write the one sentence that is not a rule for following directions.

1. Listen carefully.
2. Say the directions to yourself.
3. Look out the window.
4. If you don't understand something, ask questions.

**Introductions**    page 7

Write the letters of the introductions that are best.

5. **a.** Mother, this is Jim. He is in my class.
   **b.** Mother, meet Jim.
6. **a.** Jack Gray Eagle, this is Martin Howard.
   **b.** Jack Gray Eagle, I would like you to meet Martin Howard. Martin plays on my ball team.

**Sentences**    pages 26–27

Write only the sentences.

7. the green frogs
8. The green frogs jump high.
9. won the race
10. shiny new roller skates
11. Jan has new skates.
12. Three birds sing in the tree.
13. one very small bird

## Parts of a Sentence  page 28

Match these sentence parts. Write complete sentences.

14. Many small children     is a good place to ride.
15. My driveway     barks at us.
16. Our dog     learn to ride bikes.
17. My brother     has a red bike.

## Statements and Questions  pages 29–31

Write these sentences correctly.

18. why are you running
19. the clown fell down
20. we see the yellow lions
21. may we buy some popcorn
22. did you hear that lion roar
23. we are at the circus now
24. will you watch the show with me
25. there is the big elephant
26. i can see two black horses
27. where did the clown go
28. how do you like this circus

## Using I  pages 34–35

Write the words in ( ) that best finish each sentence.

29. (Joey and I, I and Joey) jumped in the waves.
30. Later (Fran and i, Fran and I) ran in the sand.
31. (Fran and I, I and Fran) saw a big turtle.
32. (I and Joey, Joey and I) watched the turtle swim.

# LANGUAGE
Learning About Nouns

# COMPOSITION
Writing Notes
and Letters

# STUDY SKILLS
Studying Word Meaning

# LITERATURE
Reading Poetry

Look at the pictures. You can see people and things. They are in different places.

Choose one of the pictures to talk about. Name the people you see. Where do you think they are? Name the place. Now look at the picture very closely. See how many things you can name.

Who is reading a letter in one of the pictures? Have you ever received a letter? Who was it from? In this unit you will learn how to write letters. Letters are a good way to tell other people about things you are doing.

# LANGUAGE

## Lesson 1: Naming Words for People

Study the picture. Look at the people in it.

### Think and Discuss

In the picture there are many people. They are waiting for a bus. Who is the first person in line? Who is the last person?

Some words name people. These words are called **nouns.** Match each noun below with a person in the picture.

baby    mother    boy    woman    man

### Practice

**A.** Write each word. If the word is a noun, write yes next to it. If it is not, write no.

**1.** away      **2.** farmer      **3.** did
**4.** doctor    **5.** under       **6.** teacher

**B.** Read each sentence. Write each noun.

**7.** The baby eats. **8.** The boy talks.
**9.** The woman is late. **10.** A nurse is waiting.
**11.** Is the driver new? **12.** A man reads.

## *Apply*

**C. 13.–16.** Think of people who might ride a bus. A teacher is one person. Write nouns to name four people.

# HOW OUR LANGUAGE GROWS

Are you a puppy? Are you a kitten? No, you are not. These are names for young animals. Many young animals have special names. Read the adult names and the names for young animals.

rabbit, bunny     goat, kid     owl, owlet
deer, fawn        lion, cub     kangaroo, joey

**1.** What is a young deer called? Write the name.
**2.** What is a young owl called? Write the name.

# Lesson 2: Naming Words for Places and Things

Study the picture. Find each place and thing.

house    barn    pond    duck    fence    tree

## Think and Discuss

You know that some words name people. Those words are called **nouns.** Nouns can also name places. A house is a place. People could be in a house. Name some other places where people could be.

Some words name things. A fence is a thing. A tree is a thing. Is a duck a person or a thing? Animals and plants are things. Words that name things are nouns too.

> ● A **noun** is a word that names a person, place, or thing.

## Practice

**A.** Read the sentences. Write the nouns.

1. The ocean is blue.
2. This house is small.
3. Don't forget your coat.
4. Where is my scarf?
5. The desert is hot.
6. A tent fell down.

**B.** One word in each group is not a noun. Write the three words that <u>are</u> nouns.

| | | | |
|---|---|---|---|
| **7.** park | farm | faster | rope |
| **8.** house | running | town | dress |
| **9.** begin | cap | kite | kitchen |
| **10.** fish | apple | city | sad |
| **11.** ocean | quietly | forest | tooth |
| **12.** open | frog | sock | nickel |
| **13.** clock | building | sit | chair |
| **14.** train | pretty | coat | button |
| **15.** mitten | cat | store | slowly |
| **16.** and | foot | lake | book |

## Apply

**C. 17.–20.** What could fit inside this box? Write two nouns that name things. Where could this box be? Write two nouns that name places.

## A Challenge

Read the two sentences.

I cannot <u>skate</u> today.   I lost one <u>skate</u>.

In which sentence does <u>skate</u> name a thing? What does <u>skate</u> mean in the other sentence?
Pick a word below. Write two sentences using that word. Show two ways the word can be used.

**1.** paint   **2.** laugh   **3.** brush   **4.** ring

# Lesson 3: Writing Names and Titles of People

Sandy's parents will have a party. Read the list of people to invite.

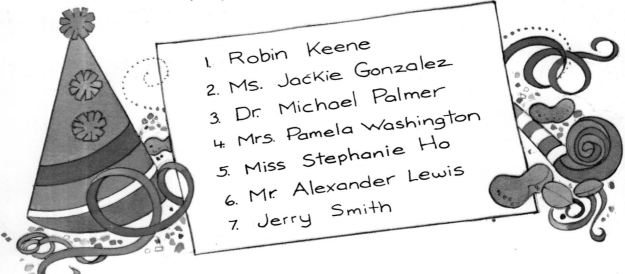

1. Robin Keene
2. Ms. Jackie Gonzalez
3. Dr. Michael Palmer
4. Mrs. Pamela Washington
5. Miss Stephanie Ho
6. Mr. Alexander Lewis
7. Jerry Smith

## Think and Discuss

Look at the list. How does each first name begin? How does each last name begin?

Look at the second name. It has a **title** in front of it. The title is <u>Ms</u>. Find the other titles. How does each title begin? Most titles end with a period. Which title has no period?

- Begin the name of a person with a capital letter.
- Begin titles of people with capital letters. Put a period after <u>Mr.</u>, <u>Mrs.</u>, <u>Ms.</u>, and <u>Dr.</u>

# Practice

**A.** Read each pair of names. Write the one that is written correctly.

**1.** eddie wall
    Eddie Wall

**2.** Ms. Ina Field
    Ms Ina Field

**B.** Write each name correctly.

**3.** miss kolk     **4.** dr kim han
**5.** mr luis rojas    **6.** mrs jones

**C. 7.–11.** Listen as your teacher reads some directions.

# Apply

**D. 12.–15.** Pretend you are making a party list. Write four names of people to invite. Put a title before each name.

### To Memorize

## Who Has Seen the Wind?

Who has seen the wind?
    Neither you nor I;
But when the trees bow down their heads
    The wind is passing by.

Christina Rossetti

Have you ever seen the wind? Have you ever heard the wind? Tell about it.

# Lesson 4: Writing Names of Places

Maya and Max are lost. Why will the police officer be able to help Maya and Max?

I live at 211 Cornell Street.

I live at 217 Cornell Street, here in Ithaca, New York.

## Think and Discuss

Nouns can name places. When they name special places, they begin with capital letters. Look back at the picture. On what street do Max and Maya live? In what city do they live? In what state do they live? All of these nouns name special places. They begin with capital letters. Notice that a comma (,) is used between the name of the city and the state.

- Begin the names of streets with capital letters.
- Begin the names of cities and states with capital letters.
- Use a comma between the name of a city and a state.

## Practice

**A.** Find the mistakes. Write each city and state name correctly.

1. Gary, indiana
2. lodi, California
3. Atlanta Georgia
4. Albany, New york
5. houston, Texas
6. Seattle Washington
7. nome, Alaska
8. Ames Iowa
9. Butte, montana
10. Jackson hole, Wyoming

**B.** Write the sentences. Begin the names of places correctly. Add commas if they are needed.

11. Maya has a friend who lives on Dryden road.
12. Dryden road crosses college avenue.
13. Leslie lives on the corner of dryden road and elmwood avenue.
14. Leslie's brother goes to school in new haven, connecticut.
15. Her sister lives in salem oregon.
16. Leslie is sending a letter to her friend in fort worth texas.
17. The friend lives at 24 riverside road.
18. Leslie hopes to visit her at camp in tulsa oklahoma.

## Apply

**C. 19.–20.** Write your address and the address of a friend. Include the street, the city, and the state.

# Lesson 5: Understanding One or More Than One

Study the pictures. Read the nouns.

cow     cows     fox     foxes

## Think and Discuss

Which nouns name one thing? Which nouns name more than one thing?

Most nouns add the letter **s** to name more than one thing. Which noun above adds **s** to name more than one?

Add **es** to nouns that end in **x, ch, sh,** or **s** to name more than one thing. Which noun above added **es**?

Now read these sentences.

1. The <u>dog</u> chased the <u>goat</u>.
2. The <u>horse</u> galloped past the <u>ranch</u>.

Look at the underlined nouns. How would you make each noun name more than one?

> • Add **s** to most nouns to mean more than one.
> • Add **es** to most nouns that end in **x, ch, sh,** or **s** to mean more than one.

## Practice

**A.** Read each pair of words. Write the noun from each pair that names more than one.

1. girls     friend
2. frame     zoos
3. axes     turkey
4. hay     dishes
5. ranchers     kitten
6. benches     pet
7. classes     school
8. doors     house
9. lake     ponds
10. bed     wishes

**B.** Write each sentence. Use the correct noun.

11. The farmer had two (cow, cows).
12. His children rode three (horse, horses).
13. They trotted through many low (bush, bushes).
14. We rode in a big (wagon, wagons).
15. We sat on six (box, boxes) in the back.

**C.** Make each noun name more than one. Write the nouns.

16. barn
17. chicken
18. glass
19. leash
20. patch
21. wish

## Apply

**D. 22.–24.** Write three sentences about a class trip to a farm. Use three of the nouns below.

tractors     classes     buses     lunches

# Lesson 6: Writing Names of Days, Months, and Holidays

Read the names of the days on the calendar.

| January | | | | | | |
|---|---|---|---|---|---|---|
| Sunday | Monday | Tuesday | Wednesday | Thursday | Friday | Saturday |
| New Year's Day 1 | 2 | 3 | 4 | 5 | 6 | 7 |

## Think and Discuss

The names of the days of the week are special nouns. They begin with capital letters. The names of the months are also special nouns. They begin with capital letters too. What month is shown on the calendar above?

January 1 is a special day. It is a holiday. Most people do not go to work or to school on that day. What is the name of the holiday that falls on January 1? Each important word in the name of a holiday begins with a capital letter.

Can you name the months of the year? In which month were you born?

> - Begin the name of a day of the week with a capital letter.
> - Begin the name of a month with a capital letter.
> - Begin each important word in the name of a holiday with a capital letter.

## Practice

**A.** Copy the sentences. Finish them with a name of a day of the week. Use the calendar to help you.

1. The first day of the week is _____.
2. The last day of the week is _____.
3. The day before Friday is _____.
4. The day after Monday is _____.
5. _____ is the day after Tuesday.

**B.** Write the names of these holidays correctly.

6. memorial day      7. flag day
8. thanksgiving      9. halloween
10. lincoln's birthday    11. labor day

**C.** Write these sentences correctly.

12. It is cold here in december.
13. Last year it snowed in october.
14. By february we were tired of the snow.
15. In march or april the first robins fly by.
16. april and may are rainy months.
17. I plant my garden in may and june.

## Apply

**D. 18.–20.** Write three sentences about your favorite month of the year.

# LANGUAGE REVIEW

**Nouns Name People**     pages 54–55

Write each noun that names a person.

1. The boy was almost late.
2. The singer is ready to begin.
3. One man claps.
4. My grandmother smiles.
5. The girl sings well.

**Nouns Name Places and Things**     pages 56–57

Write each noun that names a place or thing.

| | | | |
|---|---|---|---|
| 6. mother | river | car | girl |
| 7. book | farmer | lake | children |
| 8. actor | clown | box | airport |
| 9. dancer | tape | man | home |
| 10. artist | frog | hotel | grandfather |

**Names and Titles**     pages 58–59

Write each name correctly. Put periods where they belong.

11. carolyn weeks      12. dr neil goldman
13. miss lian wong      14. mr renaldo perez
15. ms kathy jacobs      16. alexander jones

## Names of Places    pages 60–61

Write these place names correctly. Use capital letters and commas where they are needed.

17. east avenue
18. main street
19. portland oregon
20. bangor maine
21. akron ohio
22. naples florida

## One or More Than One    pages 62–63

Change the nouns. Make them show more than one.

23. book    24. dress    25. song    26. bench
27. dish    28. bus    29. chair    30. box

## Days of the Week, Months of the Year, and Holidays    pages 64–65

Write each sentence correctly. Use capital letters where they are needed.

31. The actors came on wednesday.
32. We saw a play on labor day.
33. Last september we saw a play too.

## Applying Nouns

Draw a picture of a place. Put in people and things.

34. Write names for the people and things you draw.
35. Write a sentence to tell about the place.

# STUDY SKILLS

## Lesson 7: Understanding Synonyms

Read the two sentences below.

1. That insect is a <u>firefly</u>.
2. Yes, that insect is a <u>lightning bug</u>.

### Think and Discuss

What did one person call the insect? What did the other person call the insect?

Do <u>firefly</u> and <u>lightning bug</u> mean the same thing? These words are **synonyms.**

> ● **Synonyms** are words that mean almost the same thing.

### Practice

**A.** Find two words in each group that mean almost the same thing. Write the words.

1. paint    pail    bucket    house
2. rope    can    box    cord
3. path    new    road    girl
4. top    middle    bottom    center
5. quiet    stillness    sheep    plant

**B.** Change the underlined word. Use a word from the box that means the same thing. Write the new sentence.

| | | | |
|---|---|---|---|
| woods | car | cots | Dad |

6. Mom parked our <u>automobile</u>.
7. We were in the <u>forest</u>.
8. <u>Father</u> put up a tent.
9. That night we slept on <u>beds</u>.

## *Apply*

**C. 10.–12.** Think of a noun for each picture below. Write the word. Then talk about the words with your classmates. Find out if you wrote the same words. Find out if you wrote words that mean almost the same thing.

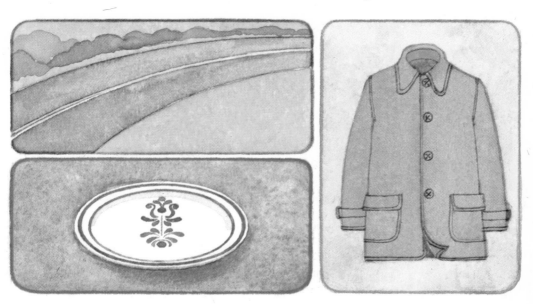

# Lesson 8: Understanding Compound Words

What do you think this machine does to words? What is happening to each pair of words?

RAIN
BOW
HOUSE
DOG
BIRTH
GOLD
DAY
FISH

RAINBOW

## Think and Discuss

Think about the small words you see. Think about what happens when they come out of the machine. Find the word <u>rain</u> and the word <u>bow</u>. Point to the new word they make together. What other words in the picture can be put together?

> ● Sometimes two words can be put together. Then they make a new word. The new word is called a **compound word.**

# Practice

**A.** Read the words below. Write each compound word you find.

| | | | |
|---|---|---|---|
| **1.** window | snowball | finger | rabbit |
| **2.** raindrop | follow | fancy | purple |
| **3.** letter | doorbell | father | middle |
| **4.** mailbox | farmer | morning | apple |

**B.** Make compound words. Write each word that has a number in front of it. Add a word from the box to it.

**5.** foot    **6.** tea    **7.** star    **8.** sea    **9.** side

| ball | shell | fish | walk | cup |
|---|---|---|---|---|

**C.** Read each group of words. Choose the two words that will make a compound. Write each compound.

| | | |
|---|---|---|
| **10.** butter | many | fly |
| **11.** grass | green | hopper |
| **12.** cook | dinner | book |
| **13.** sun | flower | color |
| **14.** fish | grand | mother |

# Apply

**D. 15.–18.** Think of four compound words you can make with <u>light</u>. <u>Flashlight</u> is one. Write the compounds.

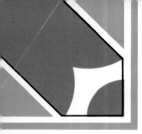

# COMPOSITION

## *Lesson 9: Writing Invitations*

Mr. John's class wanted to invite parents and friends to a picnic. Each child wrote an **invitation**. Read what Clark wrote.

**Heading** —————
**Greeting** —————

**Body** —————

**Closing** —————
**Signature** —————

> November 20, 19--
> Dear Mom,
>     Please come to our class picnic. Bring your lunch. The picnic will be at noon Monday. Meet us at Foster Park.
>                     Your son,
>                     Clark

## *Think and Discuss*

An invitation is one kind of friendly letter. It asks you to come somewhere. A friendly letter has five parts. Name the parts. Tell what is in each part. Tell where each part is written.

Where do you see commas in the invitation? Where do you see periods? Which words begin with capital letters?

- A letter has five parts: the **heading,** the **greeting,** the **body,** the **closing,** and the **signature.**
- Use a comma (,) between the day and the year in the heading. Use a comma (,) after the greeting and the closing.

## Practice

**A.** Look at this invitation. Stuart forgot some capital letters. Find his mistakes. Write the invitation correctly.

october 24, 19--

dear henry,

please come to a halloween parade. It will be after school on tuesday. Meet us at the playground.

Your friend,

Stuart

## Apply

**B.** Look at what Flo's teacher wrote on the board.

> **Who:** Anyone you want to invite
> **What:** A party to make paper snowflakes
> **When:** Thursday at 2 o'clock
> **Where:** In Room 2A

Flo wants to invite her father. Write an invitation. Write what Flo might say.

# Lesson 10: Writing Thank You Notes and Envelopes

Mr. Lane's class went to a pet store. After the trip the class wrote this note. Then they addressed the envelope.

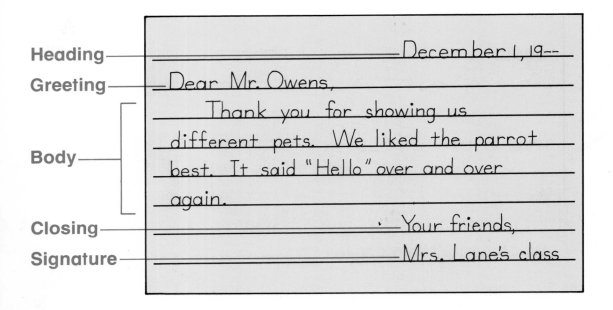

Heading ——
December 1, 19--

Greeting ——
Dear Mr. Owens,

Body ——
Thank you for showing us different pets. We liked the parrot best. It said "Hello" over and over again.

Closing ——
Your friends,

Signature ——
Mrs. Lane's class

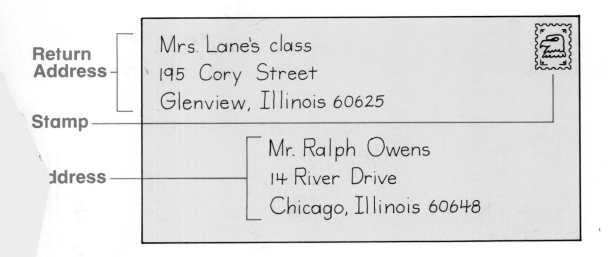

Return Address ——
Mrs. Lane's class
195 Cory Street
Glenview, Illinois 60625

Stamp ——

...dress ——
Mr. Ralph Owens
14 River Drive
Chicago, Illinois 60648

# Think and Discuss

A thank you note is another kind of friendly letter. What do you tell in a thank you note?

Look at the envelope. Find the **address**. The address tells who will receive the letter. What else does the address tell? Find the **return address**. It tells who is sending the letter.

# Practice

**A.** Write a thank you note. Use the parts below. Put each part where it belongs.

**1.** June 21, 19--  **2.** Dear Uncle Tony,

**3.** Love,  **4.** Lisa

**5.** Thank you for the fishing rod. It is a nice present. I will catch a fish for you.

# Apply

**B. 6.** Thank someone for something they gave you. Write a thank you note. Then address an envelope to that person.

# Lesson 11: Combining Sentences

Tara plans to write a letter to her friend Mark. Read what she wants to tell him.

1. Camp was fun.
2. Horses were in a barn.
3. Ponies were in a barn.
4. Ella liked to ride Red Ink.
5. I liked to ride Red Ink.

## Think and Discuss

Which words are the same in sentences 2 and 3? Which words are different? The sentences can be joined together. Try it. Use the word <u>and</u>. Say the new sentence.

Look at sentences 4 and 5. Combine the sentences into just one sentence. Say the new sentence.

Sometimes <u>and</u> can be used to put ideas from two sentences together. Tara did this in her letter to Mark.

Read the letter that Tara wrote.

---

July 12, 19--

Dear Mark,

Camp was fun. Horses and ponies were in a barn. Ella and I like to ride Red Ink.

Love,
Tara

---

## Practice

**A.** Copy the letter parts. Add the three missing commas. Write them in the correct places. Combine two sentences that are in the body. Check your work.

1. **Heading:** July 14 19--
2. **Greeting:** Dear Chris
3. **Body:** Guess what we did yesterday?
   Mona went swimming.
   I went swimming.
4. **Closing:** Love
5. **Signature:** (Write your own name.)

## Apply

**B. 6.** Write a letter to your teacher. Tell about something a friend and you did. Use the word <u>and</u> to join your friend's name and <u>I</u>.

# Lesson 12: Editing a Letter

Bert wrote a letter. Then he edited it. This means he read it again carefully. He looked for mistakes. Study the letter.

**Editing Marks**

≡ capitalize

⊙ make a period

∧ add something

⋏ add a comma

⌐ take something away

◯ spell correctly

⁋ indent the paragraph

January 10, 19--

Dear
~~Deer~~ Dick,

    I am glad you can come for a
visit
~~vizit~~. Please come next ~~Fryday~~ Friday. We
meet
will ~~meat~~ at the corner. Take the
off
number 12 bus. Get ~~of~~ at Brewster
Street.

Your ~~freind~~ friend,

Bert

## Think and Discuss

Bert found some mistakes in spelling. He put circles around those words. What did he do to show the correct spelling?

He used this mark ⋏ to show where commas must be added. Where did he add commas? Now Bert will write the letter correctly.

## Practice

**A.** Copy Bert's letter correctly. Use the changes he made.

## Apply

**B.** Look at the letter you wrote in Lesson 11. Did you use commas? Edit your letter for spelling mistakes. Then write it correctly.

---

# MECHANICS PRACTICE

### Writing Names and Dates

● Begin the names of people and places with capital letters.
● Begin the names of days, months, and holidays with capital letters.
● Put a period (.) after these titles: <u>Mr.</u>, <u>Mrs.</u>, <u>Ms.</u>, <u>Dr.</u>
● Put a comma (,) between the name of a city and a state.
● Put a comma (,) between the day of the month and the year.

Write these sentences correctly.

1. Did jan call phil?
2. Ms perin wrote a book.
3. monday is labor day.
4. Where is hill street?
5. Is this dallas texas?
6. Today is april 1 19--.

# LITERATURE

## Lesson 13: Reading Poetry

Look at the picture. Read what one poet wrote.

### First Snow

Snow makes whiteness where it falls.
The bushes look like popcorn-balls.
And places where I always play,
Look like somewhere else today.

Mary Louise Allen

### Think and Discuss

A poem can paint a picture. Look again at what the poet wrote. What color did everything turn? What looked like popcorn-balls?

### Practice

**A.** Write the sentence that describes the picture painted in the poem.

1. Bushes were covered with popcorn-balls.
2. Popcorn-balls looked cold and wet.
3. Snow on bushes looked like popcorn-balls.

## *Apply*

**B. 4.** Read the poem. Try to see the picture it paints. Write a sentence to tell about it.

### Brooms

On stormy days
    When the wind is high
Tall trees are brooms
    Sweeping the sky.
They swish their branches
    In buckets of rain,
And swash and sweep it
    Blue again.

Dorothy Aldis

## A BOOK TO READ

Title: **Whose Cat Is That?**
Author: Virginia Kahl
Publisher: Charles Scribner's Sons

A small white cat was looking for a home. At the first house a kind lady fixed it a bowl of cream. She named the kitten Melinda. The kitten went next door. A boy fed it fish and named it Miranda! Read what happened after that.

# 3 UNIT TEST

● **Nouns**  pages 54–57

Write the noun in each sentence.

**1.** A town is near.   **2.** This ranch is big.
**3.** A man rides by.   **4.** His horse is brown.

● **Names of People and Places**  pages 58–61

Write the sentences correctly. Use capital letters and commas where needed.

**5.** mr clark lives on mill road in denver colorado.
**6.** miss tracy hays visited plains georgia.

● **One or More Than One**  pages 62–63

Write the noun in each group that means more than one.

**7.** boots, bell   **8.** hat, foxes   **9.** wishes, dress

● **Names of Days, Months, and Holidays**  pages 64–65

Write the sentence correctly.

**10.** thanksgiving is the last thursday in november.

● **Synonyms**  pages 68–69

Write the two words in each group that mean almost the same thing.

**1.** night   day   evening   **2.** woods   forest   bush

## Compound Words   pages 70–71

Make four compound words. Match each word in the box with one of the words below it. Write the new words.

| cow | out | rain | barn |
|-----|-----|------|------|

**3.** side     **4.** boy     **5.** yard     **6.** drop

## Writing and Editing Letters   pages 72–79

Write a thank you letter. Use the parts below. Remember to edit your writing.

**1.** February 18, 19--           **2.** Dear Len,
**3.** Your friend,              **4.** (Your own name)
**5.** Thank you for the game.

## Combining Sentences   pages 76–77

Make one sentence from the two given.

**6.** The barns are red.     The fences are red.

## Literature   pages 80–81

Read the poem. Write the part that describes the trees.

The fenceposts wear marshmallow hats
On a snowy day;
Bushes in their nightgowns
Are kneeling down to pray—
And all the trees have silver skirts
And want to dance away.

Dorothy Aldis

# LANGUAGE
## Learning About Verbs
# COMPOSITION
## Writing Sentences

# STUDY SKILLS
## Using Books
# LITERATURE
## Reading a True Story

Think about your trip to school today. Did you and a friend <u>walk</u> to school? Did you <u>come</u> in a bus? Or did you <u>ride</u> your bike?

Read the underlined words above. These words are action words. They tell what someone or something is doing.

Talk about the people in one of the pictures. Make up sentences that have interesting action words. Use them to tell what is happening in the picture.

Use different action words to tell about the other pictures. Which action words tell about things <u>you</u> like to do?

# LANGUAGE

## Lesson 1: Understanding Verbs

Read the poem about feet.

### Feet

Feet are very special things
For special kinds of fun.
On weekdays they walk off to school
Or skip—hop—or run—
On Saturdays they roller-skate
Or bicycle—or hike—
On Sundays they just do the things
That other people like.

Myra Cohn Livingston

### *Think and Discuss*

Which four words tell what feet do on weekdays? Which three words tell what feet do on Saturdays?

The words you named show actions. They are called **action verbs.**

> ● An **action verb** is a word that shows action.

## Practice

**A.** Read the sentences. Write the verbs.

1. Chris skips to school.
2. Sometimes I jog.
3. Jan climbs trees.
4. We sit on branches.
5. The baby crawls.
6. She drinks milk.

**B.** Choose a verb from the box for each sentence. Then write the sentence.

| dance | kick | jump | march |

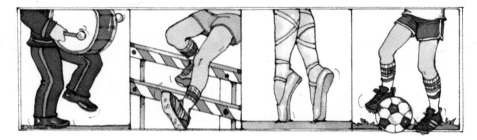

7. Some feet _____ in a parade.
8. How high these feet _____ over the fence.
9. Some feet _____ on their toes.
10. Those feet _____ the ball.

## Apply

**C.** **11.–12.** Think of actions you do with your feet. Write two statements. Use interesting action verbs.

# Lesson 2: Understanding Verbs That Tell About Now

Look at the picture. Read the sentences.

1. Jim and Sid <u>find</u> shells.
2. Gwen <u>finds</u> a starfish.

## Think and Discuss

What are the verbs in sentences 1 and 2? Do they tell about action that happens now or in the past?

Sentence 1 tells about two children. The verb <u>find</u> is used in the sentence. Sentence 2 tells about one person. The verb <u>finds</u> is used. How is <u>finds</u> different from <u>find</u>?

> ● Add **s** to an action verb that tells about one person or thing.

## Practice

**A.** Write the action verbs that tell about now.

1. Gisela jumps over a log.
2. Sid runs after Francesca.
3. Gisela and Sid chase me.
4. Some girls swim with Muna.

**B.** Choose the correct verb. Write the sentences.

5. The boys (skip, skips) together.
6. Their mother (wave, waves) to them.
7. Gwen (hide, hides) the ball.
8. Her friends (play, plays) with her.

## *Apply*

**C.** Look around your classroom. Write four sentences. Choose one verb from each group below. Tell what your classmates are doing now.

9. write, writes
10. take, takes
11. ask, asks
12. look, looks

# HOW OUR LANGUAGE GROWS

Many people work to keep others safe and healthy. These people have special names. Read them.

dentist    fire fighter    police officer
doctor     nurse    crossing guard

1. What does each person above do? How could you find out?
2. Think of two more important jobs. Write the special names for the workers.

# Lesson 3: Understanding Verbs That Tell About the Past

Read the sentences Vicki wrote.

> My Bad Day
> Saturday we played in the park.
> I climbed a fence and acted silly.
> Then I learned a lesson.

## Think and Discuss

Vicki told about something that happened in the past. Name the four action verbs in the sentences. Which two letters are at the end of each verb?

> ● **Verbs** can tell about action in the past. Form the past time of most verbs by adding **ed.**

## Practice

**A.** Write each verb that tells about the past.

1. Vicki's big brother helped her.
2. He picked her up.
3. They rushed home.

**4.** They talked to the doctor.

**5.** Dr. Ramos looked at her arm.

**6.** She smiled at her.

**B.** Finish each sentence. Choose a verb from the box.

| | | | | |
|---|---|---|---|---|
| acted | needed | cleaned | showed | folded |

**7.** The doctor _____ her arm.

**8.** Vicki _____ an X ray.

**9.** Dr. Ramos _____ a sling for Vicki.

**10.** Vicki _____ it to her brother.

**11.** Vicki _____ very brave.

## Apply

**C. 12.–15.** Tell about a time you visited a doctor. Write four sentences. Use verbs that tell about the past.

**To Memorize**

To give — and forgive —
Is a good way to live.

Louis Untermeyer

What does <u>forgive</u> mean? Do you believe what the poem says? Tell why or why not.

# Lesson 4: Using Forms of <u>Be</u>

Some verbs do not show action. Read these sentences.

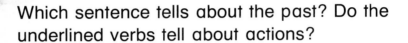

1. All morning Chris <u>was</u> busy.
2. Now Chris <u>is</u> tired.

Which sentence tells about the past? Do the underlined verbs tell about actions?

## Think and Discuss

The underlined verbs tell what Chris <u>is</u> and <u>was</u>. They tell about <u>being</u>.

Read these sentences.

3. I <u>am</u> in the tree.
4. I <u>was</u> in the tree.
5. Hal <u>is</u> on the ground.
6. Hal <u>was</u> on the ground.
7. Apples <u>are</u> on the branch.
8. Apples <u>were</u> on the branch.

Sentences 3, 5, and 7 tell about now. Sentences 4, 6, and 8 tell about the past. Which two verbs are used with the word <u>I</u>? Which verbs are used with one person or thing? Which verbs are used with more than one person or thing?

| **Present** | **Past** |
|---|---|
| am, is, are | was, were |

## *Practice*

**A.** Copy each sentence. Underline the verb.

1. I am under the tree.
2. Hal is my best friend.
3. Children are in the orchard with me.
4. They are very happy.
5. We were very busy today.
6. Soon lunch was ready.

**B.** Choose the correct verb. Write the sentences.

7. Mary (is, am) with us.
8. Her brothers (is, are) here too.
9. Jo and Ed (was, were) busy.
10. Apples (is, are) very good for you.
11. I (was, were) high up in the tree.
12. The tree (is, am) easy to climb.
13. I (am, is) not in the tree now.

## *Apply*

**C. 14.–15.** Look at the chart on this page. Pick one verb that tells about now and one verb that tells about the past. Use the verbs in sentences of your own.

# Lesson 5: Using Forms of _Have_

Read what these children are saying.

We had an umbrella last year.

Howard has a funny hat.

We all have wet feet.

I have a very long raincoat.

## Think and Discuss

Look back at the underlined verbs. Which verb tells about the past? Which verbs tell about now? Use <u>has</u> with one person or thing. Use <u>have</u> with more than one person or thing.

Look at Howard's sentences. Did he use <u>have</u> or <u>has</u> to go with the word <u>I</u>?

This chart will help you with your work.

| Present | Past |
|---|---|
| have, has | had |

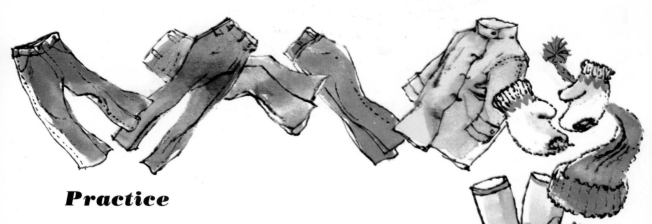

## Practice

**A.** Copy each sentence. Underline the verb.

1. Floyd has four pairs of pants.
2. We have green and yellow running shoes.
3. I had a yellow raincoat last year.
4. My mittens have holes in them.

**B.** Choose the correct verb. Write the sentences.

5. Ana (has, have) a blue hat.
6. Last fall Ana (have, had) boots.
7. Ed and Nina (has, have) new socks.
8. Floyd (have, had) a brown coat.
9. Some coats (has, have) hoods.
10. Earl (has, have) a new belt.
11. All my friends (has, have) book bags.
12. The players (has, had) numbers on their shirts.

## Apply

**C. 13.–14.** Look at the chart in this lesson. Pick one verb that shows present time. Write a sentence with that verb. Then write your sentence again. This time make it tell about the past.

# Lesson 6: Understanding Contractions

Read these sentences.

1. That food <u>is</u> for you, Rex.
2. My food <u>is not</u> for you.
3. You <u>have not</u> finished your food.

Which food may Rex eat?

## Think and Discuss

The word <u>not</u> may be used next to a verb. It changes the meaning of the sentence.

Look at sentences 2 and 3. They can be written a different way. Read these sentences.

4. My food <u>isn't</u> for you.
5. You <u>haven't</u> finished your food.

<u>Isn't</u> and <u>haven't</u> are **contractions.** They are short ways of saying <u>is not</u> and <u>have not</u>. The letter **o** is left out of <u>not</u> in these contractions. A mark takes the place of the letter **o.** This mark (') is called an **apostrophe.**

Here is a list of some common contractions.

| | |
|---|---|
| is + not = isn't | was + not = wasn't |
| are + not = aren't | were + not = weren't |
| have + not = haven't | had + not = hadn't |
| has + not = hasn't | |

What letter is left out of the contraction <u>wasn't</u>?
What two words make up the contraction <u>hadn't</u>?

## *Practice*

**A.** Study the sentences below. Then close your book. Take out a piece of paper. Write the sentences as your teacher reads them. Remember to begin and end your sentences correctly.

1. My dog isn't very smart.
2. He hasn't had any lessons.
3. Dogs aren't hard to train.
4. Rex wasn't a good learner.

**B.** Use contractions in place of the underlined words. Write the sentences.

5. Rex <u>has not</u> had his bath.
6. He <u>was not</u> in the yard.
7. Rex <u>is not</u> in the house.
8. We <u>had not</u> seen him at all.
9. We <u>are not</u> very pleased with Rex.

## *Apply*

**C. 10.–14.** Write five sentences about pets. Use five contractions from the list in this lesson.

# Lesson 7: Using the Verbs
## Go, Come, and Run

Some action verbs do not add **ed.** They tell about the past in a different way. Read these sentences.

1. The riders <u>go</u> down the hill.
2. Barbara <u>goes</u> down the hill.
3. Marv <u>went</u> down the hill already.

Which sentence tells about the past?

## Think and Discuss

Sentences 1 and 2 tell about things that are happening now. Which verb is used with one person or thing? Which verb is used with more than one person or thing? Sentence 3 tells about the past. Which verb is used?

Now read these sentences. Tell the verb in each sentence.

4. Dogs run.    5. A dog runs.    6. Dogs ran.
7. People come.   8. Diego comes.   9. Diego came.

The verbs <u>go</u>, <u>run</u>, and <u>come</u> change their spellings to tell about the past. The chart on the next page will help you with your work.

| Present | Past |
|---|---|
| go, goes | went |
| come, comes | came |
| run, runs | ran |

## Practice

**A.** Copy each sentence. Underline the verb. Does each sentence tell about <u>now</u> or the <u>past</u>? Write <u>now</u> or <u>past</u> after each one.

1. A puppy runs after Barbara.
2. Marv came to the top of the hill.
3. A dog went up to him.

**B.** Change the underlined verb. Make each sentence tell about the past. Write the sentences.

4. Barbara <u>goes</u> very fast.
5. She <u>comes</u> around a sharp corner.

**C.** Change the underlined verb. Make each sentence tell about now. Write the sentences.

6. One dog <u>ran</u> past Marv.
7. Marv <u>went</u> by us quickly.

## Apply

**D. 8.–12.** Choose five verbs from the chart in this lesson. Use each of them in a sentence.

# LANGUAGE REVIEW

**Verbs**   pages 86–87

Copy the sentences. Underline the verbs.

1. Jean hops on one foot.
2. Mike follows her.
3. Sue and Juan run by me.
4. Boys wave to them.

**Verbs That Tell About Now**   pages 88–89

Choose the correct verb. Write the sentences.

5. My uncle often (visit, visits) us.
6. The boys and girls (ask, asks) him questions.
7. He (work, works) on a tugboat.

**Verbs That Tell About the Past**   pages 90–91

Make each sentence tell about the past. Choose the correct verb. Write the sentences.

8. Mrs. Jackson (calls, called) Vicki.
9. The family (walks, walked) to the beach.
10. Mom and Dad (splashed, splash) the girls.

**Forms of <u>Be</u>**   pages 92–93

Choose the correct verb. Write the sentences.

11. Brenda (is, are) my sister.
12. I (is, am) her brother.
13. Chris (was, were) our neighbor.
14. Her parents (was, were) nice to us.

## Forms of <u>Have</u>    pages 94–95

Choose the correct verb. Write the sentences.

**15.** Rita (has, have) a party every spring.
**16.** I always (has, have) a good time there.
**17.** My friends (has, have) fun too.
**18.** Rita (have, had) a big party this year.
**19.** All of her guests (has, had) fun.

## Contractions    pages 96–97

Write a contraction for each pair of words.

**20.**  has  +  not  =  _____
**21.** were  +  not  =  _____
**22.** was  +  not  =  _____
**23.**   is  +  not  =  _____

## Forms of <u>Go</u>, <u>Run</u>, and <u>Come</u>    pages 98–99

Copy each sentence. Underline the verbs. Does each sentence tell about <u>now</u> or the <u>past</u>? Write <u>now</u> or <u>past</u> after each one.

**24.** George ran to the mailbox.
**25.** The mail came early.
**26.** George goes back inside.

## Applying Verbs

**27.–30.** Think of two verbs that tell about now. Think of two verbs that tell about the past. Use the verbs in sentences.

# STUDY SKILLS

## Lesson 8: Using the Dictionary

Li does not know what the word <u>echo</u> means. She will use a dictionary to find out.

### Think and Discuss

Li looks at this dictionary page.

eaves      230      **eddy**

**eaves** [ēvz] The lower edge of a roof that hangs over the side of the building.

**e·col·o·gy** [e·kol′-ə-jē] A science that studies how life forms live together.

The words at the top of the page are **guide words.** They tell Li that <u>eaves</u> is the first word on page 230. <u>Eddy</u> is the last word on this page. Does <u>echo</u> come between <u>eaves</u> and <u>eddy</u> in ABC order? <u>Echo</u> must be on this page.

Read this dictionary entry for <u>echo</u>.

**echo** (ekō) **1.** A sound that bounces back to its starting point. **2.** To repeat the sound of.

The word in dark type is the entry word. Some entry words have more than one meaning. Each number shows a different meaning. How many meanings are given for <u>echo</u>?

# *Practice*

**A.** Read the guide words on the left. Write the word that would be on the same page as the guide words.

1. **do–dull**        dig        drag        desk
2. **plant–pull**        pinch        paint        poke
3. **game–give**        get        gum        go

**B.** Read the dictionary entry. Answer the questions.

**safe** (sāf) **1.** Free from danger or evil. **2.** Unhurt. **3.** A strong metal box for protecting things. **4.** In baseball, to reach base without being put out.

4. How many meanings are listed for this word?
5. What is the entry word?
6. What does meaning 2 say?
7. Which meaning matches the picture?

# *Apply*

**C. 8.–10.** Look up <u>coat</u>, <u>fall</u>, and <u>raise</u> in your dictionary. Write one meaning for each.

## *A Challenge*

Use a dictionary. Look up the underlined words. Then answer each question.

1. Can a <u>seahorse</u> <u>gallop</u>?
2. Will a <u>goblet</u> <u>frighten</u> you?

# Lesson 9: Using a Telephone Book

Ms. Perez wants to call her friend Fred. She does not know his telephone number. She can find Fred's number in the telephone book.

The telephone book lists people's last names in ABC order. Fred's last name is <u>Rice</u>. Under what letter should Ms. Perez look?

## Think and Discuss

Ms. Perez looked on this page.

| Reston | Russell |
|---|---|
| **Reston, Paul** 6 Main Street.....255-0622 | **Roy, Jane** 4 Day Road.........285-0855 |
| **Rhett, Doris** 9 Day Road.......266-9056 | **Rush, Dan** 23 Fry Lane.......265-9075 |
| **Rice, Fred** 65 Owl Lane.......465-0846 | **Rusk, Melba** 1 Sims Road.....255-1777 |

The two words at the top of the page are **guide words.** They tell the first and the last names on a page. What is the first name that would be listed on this page?

<u>Rice</u> comes between <u>Reston</u> and <u>Russell</u> in ABC order. Find the listing for Fred Rice. His last name comes first in the listing. The listing gives his address and telephone number. What is Fred's address? What is his telephone number?

Look at the other listings on the page. Which two people live on the same street?

# Practice

**A.** Answer these questions. Use the telephone book page in this lesson.

1. What is Jane Roy's telephone number?
2. What is Dan Rush's address?
3. Who lives on Main Street?
4. What is Doris Rhett's telephone number?
5. Who lives at 4 Day Road?

**B.** Use these guide words to answer the questions below.

### Baker       Bollard

6. Would Judy Black be listed on the same page as these guide words?
7. Would Mickey Chavez be listed here?
8. Would Katy Bell be listed here?
9. Would Jan Bravetree be listed here?

# Apply

**C. 10.** Make your own telephone book page. Write the listings below in ABC order. Make up addresses and telephone numbers for those that are missing. Decide which last names should be the guide words. Add them at the top of your page.

**Cott, Sid**    42 York Street . . . 888-9203
**Cruz, Elena**    _____ . . . 876-9334
**Chu, June**    87 Park Lane . . . _____
**Clyde, Bill**    _____ . . . 922-2207

# COMPOSITION

## Lesson 10: Choosing Interesting Verbs

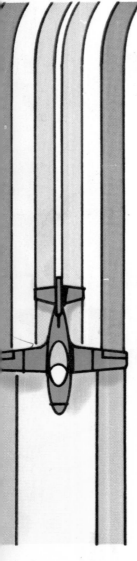

Read the three sentences. Each verb changes the picture you get of a plane.

1. The plane moves down the runway.
2. The plane zooms down the runway.
3. The plane bumps down the runway.

### Think and Discuss

The verb <u>moves</u> is not a very interesting verb. It does not give a good picture of the plane's action.

Name the verbs in sentences 2 and 3. Do these verbs help you see how the plane moves? Verbs like <u>zoom</u> and <u>bump</u> are interesting verbs.

When you write, try to use interesting verbs in your sentences. Choose verbs that say just what you want your readers to see.

### Practice

**A.** Pick the more interesting sentence in each pair. Write **a** or **b**. Then copy the verb in that sentence.

1. **a.** Mark told the secret.
   **b.** Mark whispered the secret.

2. **a.** The ball sails over the fence.
   **b.** The ball goes over the fence.

**B.** Choose the verb in ( ) that is more interesting. Write that verb.

3. Hugh (uses, pounds) the drums.
4. Jane (looked, stared) at the strange animals.
5. Pedro (strolled, came) down the path.
6. The cat (raced, went) up the tree.
7. I (put, arranged) the flowers in the vase.
8. The deer (darted, ran) away quickly.

**C.** Read the sentences. Choose verbs from the box to use in place of the underlined verbs. Write each sentence with the verb you choose.

| | | |
|---|---|---|
| trailed | leaped | speeds |
| tumbled | noticed | trapped |

9. The car <u>runs</u> along.
10. I <u>got</u> the insect.
11. I <u>saw</u> that the buds had opened.
12. A rock <u>fell</u> down the mountain.
13. The tiger <u>jumped</u> from the tree.
14. My little brother <u>came</u> behind me.

## *Apply*

**D. 15.–18.** Write four sentences about these people and things. Use interesting verbs.

trucks     a dancer     a baby     a horse

# Lesson 11: Editing Sentences

David wrote some sentences about a race. Then he edited them. Read his sentences.

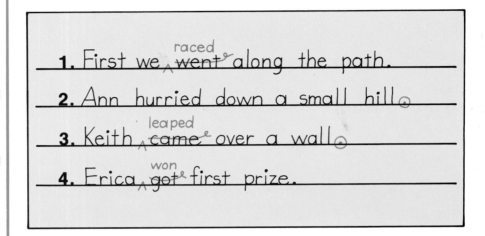

1. First we ~~went~~ ∧raced along the path.
2. Ann hurried down a small hill⊙
3. Keith ∧leaped ~~came~~ over a wall⊙
4. Erica ∧won ~~got~~ first prize.

## Think and Discuss

David used this editing mark ˞ to take away some words. What verbs did David take away? He used this mark ∧ to add some verbs. What verbs did he add? Why do you think he changed some verbs?

Look at sentence 2. Where did David use an editing mark? This mark ⊙ means to make a period. Find another sentence where a period was added.

How did editing make David's sentences better? Now he will copy the sentences using the changes he made.

## Practice

**A.** Copy David's sentences over correctly.

# *Apply*

**B.** Look back at the sentences you wrote in Lesson 10. Did you begin and end each sentence correctly? Could you change any words to make the sentences more interesting? Use editing marks to correct your sentences. Then write each sentence again.

## MECHANICS PRACTICE

### Writing Contractions

● Use an **apostrophe** (') to show that one or more letters have been left out in a contraction.

Write these sentences correctly. Add an apostrophe each time it is needed.

1. Jim hadnt ever been to the zoo.
2. He wasnt happy about that.
3. I havent been to the Bronx Zoo.
4. It isnt far away.
5. Jim hasnt been there either.
6. It isnt hard to get there.
7. We werent able to go alone.
8. Our parents arent able to take us.
9. We havent got a subway map.
10. We arent going to get there today.

# LITERATURE

## Lesson 12: Reading a True Story

True stories tell about things that really happened. Follow along as your teacher reads this true story aloud. Find out why Jumbo was "King of the Circus."

### Jumbo
### King of the Circus

by D. A. Woodliff

In 1863 a baby elephant, not yet 5 feet tall, arrived at the Paris Zoo. His name was Jumbo. When Jumbo was 4 years old, he was traded to the London Zoo. Jumbo was very ill by the time he reached London. Matthew Scott, a zookeeper, was asked to care for him. Scott spent months taking care of the elephant. He nursed Jumbo back to health.

Jumbo grew to be the largest elephant ever to be kept in captivity. He was 11½ feet tall. He weighed nearly 14,000 pounds!

Jumbo became the most famous elephant of all time. People began to use his name to mean anything of great size. <u>Jumbo</u> became a word in dictionaries.

## Jumbo Comes to the United States

An American showman named P. T. Barnum wanted to buy Jumbo for his circus. The London Zoo accepted Barnum's $10,000 offer.

P. T. Barnum hired Matthew Scott to be Jumbo's keeper in the United States. Scott led Jumbo into the traveling cage on March 15, 1882. They sailed across the Atlantic Ocean on a ship. Scott spent most of the trip at Jumbo's cage. He held the great animal's trunk.

The two arrived in New York. Thousands of people came to see this huge elephant. Jumbo led the circus parades waving a large American flag. The crowds loved him.

## Jumbo Travels with the Circus

Jumbo traveled in his own red-and-gold railway car. It was called "Jumbo's Palace Car." Matthew Scott had a high bed near the elephant's head. There was a small door

there. Jumbo wouldn't allow this door to be closed. He would reach his trunk through it for a pat from Scott. When Jumbo felt playful, he would pull blankets from Scott's bed.

Jumbo was only 24 years old when he died. This is a young age for an elephant. He had just finished a performance. He was being led back to his car along the train tracks. It was a dark September night in 1885. Jumbo was hit by a freight train. Scott was very sad when his animal friend died.

Jumbo was the most famous elephant of all time. He is remembered on both sides of the Atlantic Ocean. He was a favorite pet in the London Zoo. In America he was the star of the circus.

## Think and Discuss

A story usually has people or animals or both in it. These are called the **characters** in the story. Things happen in a story. This is called the **plot.** A story must take place somewhere. This is called the **setting.**

Name two characters in this story. Name the two places where Jumbo spent most of his life. Tell some things that happened in this true story.

## Practice

**A.** Answer these questions. Use complete sentences.

1. What is the name of the most important character?
2. What does the word <u>jumbo</u> mean today?
3. Where did people see Jumbo in London?
4. Where did people see Jumbo in the U.S.A.?
5. What happened at the end of the story?

## Apply

**B. 6.–8.** Think of a story you have read. Write three sentences. Tell who was in the story. Tell the setting for the story. Tell something that happened in the plot.

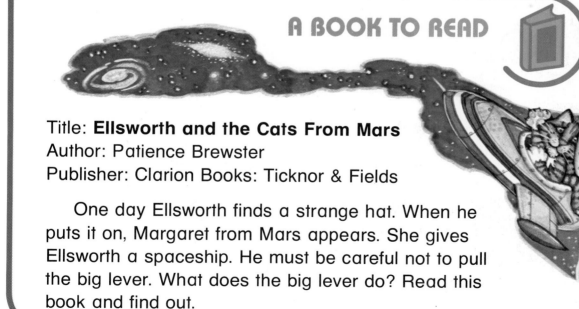

## A BOOK TO READ

Title: **Ellsworth and the Cats From Mars**
Author: Patience Brewster
Publisher: Clarion Books: Ticknor & Fields

One day Ellsworth finds a strange hat. When he puts it on, Margaret from Mars appears. She gives Ellsworth a spaceship. He must be careful not to pull the big lever. What does the big lever do? Read this book and find out.

# 4 UNIT TEST

● **Verbs**    pages 86–87

Write the letter that is under each verb.

**1.** Matt shakes his bank.    **2.** Dimes jingle inside it.
      a    b    c          a    b    c

● **Verbs That Tell About Now
or the Past**    pages 88–91, 98–99

Copy each sentence. Underline the verb. Write <u>now</u> if
the sentence tells about now. Write <u>past</u> if it tells about
the past.

**3.** Marty throws a ball.    **4.** Sara went to camp.
**5.** We ran in a race.       **6.** I looked at Ana.
**7.** They come home.         **8.** He goes to class.

● **Forms of <u>Be</u> and <u>Have</u>**    pages 92–95

Choose the correct verb. Write the sentences.

**9.** I (is, am) outside now.
**10.** Jo (has, have) her gloves on her hands.
**11.** She (is, am) a bit chilly.
**12.** Our friends (has, have) on winter coats.

● **Contractions**    pages 96–97

Write the contraction for each pair of words.

**13.** is + not = _____    **14.** had + not = _____

## The Dictionary    pages 102–103

Read the entry. Answer the questions below.

> **print** (print) 1. Letters or words marked on paper with ink. 2. Cloth stamped with a design. 3. To produce a book or newspaper.

1. How many meanings are listed for <u>print</u>?
2. Which meaning tells about cloth?
3. Could this entry be on the same page as the guide words play–put?

## Telephone Book    pages 104–105

Read the listings. Answer the questions below.

> **Todd, Sam**    5 Valley Road. . . . .947-9233
> **Torres, Vi**    423 Main Street. . .876-8304

4. What is Sam Todd's telephone number?
5. Who lives at 423 Main Street?

## Choosing Verbs and Editing Sentences    pages 106–109

Choose the most interesting verb in each pair. Write the verbs in sentences. Then edit your sentences for mistakes.

1. said, shouted     2. moves, dances

## Reading a True Story    pages 110–113

Answer these questions in complete sentences.

1. What is a true story?
2. What is the plot of a story?

# MAINTENANCE and REVIEW

**Introductions**   page 7

Write the letters of the introductions that are best.

1. **a.** Dad, this is Jane. She lives next door.
   **b.** Jane, meet my father.

2. **a.** Nita, I want you to meet Dave.
   **b.** Nita, meet Dave Owens. He is in second grade.

**Statements or Questions**   pages 29–31

Write these sentences correctly. Add periods (**.**) or question marks (**?**).

3. I am walking the dog
4. Will you come with us
5. We will go to the park
6. It is a warm night
7. Do you have a dog
8. Where do you walk it

**Nouns**   pages 54–57

Write the noun from each sentence.

9. The funny clown sang.
10. A brown pony jumped.
11. The tent was very big.
12. A little boy cheered.

**Names and Titles**   pages 58–59

Write each sentence correctly.

13. dr johns lives in boston.
14. kim lives on gar street.
15. boston is a city in massachusetts.

## One or More Than One    pages 62–63

Write two nouns from each group that tell about more than one.

**16.** eggs    farmer    benches
**17.** zoo    boxes    bushes

## Verbs    pages 86–87

Write the verb from each sentence.

**18.** The bus rumbled down the street.
**19.** Maria chased the big blue bus.

## Verbs That Tell About Now or the Past    pages 88–91

Write <u>now</u> if the underlined verb tells about now.
Write <u>past</u> if it tells about the past.

**20.** Rabbits <u>jumped</u> by.        **21.** Two girls <u>play</u>.
**22.** One frog <u>hops</u>.        **23.** Jay <u>climbed</u> the tree.

## Forms of <u>Be</u> and <u>Have</u>    pages 92–95

Choose the correct verb in (  ). Write the sentences.

**24.** I (have, has) a new baseball glove.
**25.** Cindy (is, are) a good baseball player.

## Contractions    pages 96–97

Write these contractions correctly.

**26.** arent    **27.** hasnt    **28.** werent

# LANGUAGE
Learning
About Paragraphs

# COMPOSITION
Writing a
One-Paragraph Story

# STUDY SKILLS
Studying
Word Meaning

# LITERATURE
Reading a Tale

Everyone likes stories. Some stories are make-believe. They cannot happen in real life. Other stories tell about real people and things. What is your favorite story? Who is it about? Where does the story take place?

People have many ways to tell stories. Look at the pictures. Which people are telling stories? Which people are listening to stories?

In this unit you will learn to write sentences that tell about one main idea. Think of a main idea for one of the pictures. Then tell a story about the picture. Be sure your story has a beginning, a middle, and an end.

# LANGUAGE

## Lesson 1: Understanding Paragraphs

Read the sentences. They tell about circus animals.

Circus animals do many tricks. Elephants stand on their heads. Lions sit on chairs. Horses dance in a circle.

### Think and Discuss

The sentences you read tell about one idea. That one idea is called the **main idea.** What is the main idea?

Sentences that have the same main idea are grouped together. The group of sentences is called a **paragraph.**

The first line of a paragraph begins a little to the right. It is **indented.** Read the first line of the paragraph.

- A **paragraph** is a group of sentences that tell about one main idea.
- The first line of a paragraph is **indented.**

## Practice

**A. 1.** Copy the paragraph about circus animals. Remember to indent the first line.

**B.** Read each paragraph. Choose the main idea. Write it down.

**2.**    Circus clowns look funny. They paint their faces. Some clowns wear an orange wig. Other clowns wear big shoes.
  **a.** clowns wear wigs
  **b.** clowns look funny

**3.**    Circuses travel to many cities. Some circuses travel by truck. Other circuses travel by train.
  **a.** circuses travel a lot
  **b.** circuses travel by train

**4.**    Every circus begins with a parade. The circus band plays lively music. Circus performers and animals march.
  **a.** circus parades
  **b.** animals march in parades

## Apply

**C.** Read the paragraph. Write down the main idea.

**5.**    There have been many famous circus stars. Clyde Beatty was a famous animal trainer. Emmett Kelley was a well-known clown. Antoinette Concello was a famous flyer.

# Lesson 2: Beginning a Paragraph

There are many things to tell about clocks. Read the paragraph. Think of the main idea.

Clocks come in all shapes and sizes. Some clocks are round. Clocks can also be square. Some clocks are big. Other clocks are small.

## Think and Discuss

What is the main idea of the paragraph about clocks? One sentence of the paragraph tells the main idea. It is the first sentence. Read the first sentence again.

The first sentence of a paragraph often tells the main idea. The other sentences tell about the main idea.

## Practice

**A.** Copy the paragraphs. Underline the sentence that tells the main idea.

1. Some clocks have gongs. They strike on each hour of the day. The gongs tell people what time it is.

2. Many clocks are made each year. People in Switzerland make some. Workers in Japan and the United States also make many kinds of clocks.

**3.** The first clock was made long ago. The clock did not have hands. It told time by ringing a bell.

**4.** Alarm clocks are special clocks. People set them to ring at a certain time. Alarm clocks wake people each morning.

## *Apply*

**B. 5.** Look at the watches. Think of a main idea for a paragraph about them. Write a sentence that tells the main idea.

## HOW OUR LANGUAGE GROWS

What is your name? Names have been used for a long time. Many names come from other languages. Sarah and Philip are old names. Sarah comes from the Hebrew language. It means "princess." Philip comes from the Greek language. It means "lover of horses."

1. Ask your family about your name. What does it mean? What language does it come from?
2. Make a class name chart. Write each first name. Write the language it comes from. Write what each name means.

# Lesson 3: Keeping to the Main Idea

Mrs. Wong's class is making a list. The class is listing sports. Read the list. Does every word name a sport?

| | | | |
|---|---|---|---|
| football | swimming | friend | baseball |

## Think and Discuss

Sports is the main idea of the list. Which word does not tell about the main idea?

Every paragraph has a main idea. Each sentence of a paragraph tells about it. Read the paragraph below. Something is wrong with it.

Pat plays baseball. She is a very good player. Once she hit a home run. The sun was shining.

What is the main idea of this paragraph? Which sentence does not tell about the main idea?

## Practice

A. 1. Copy the paragraph about Pat. Take out the sentence that does not belong.

**B.** Read each paragraph. Write the sentence that does not tell about the main idea.

2.     Our school has a swim team. The water is cold. The team races every Saturday. Six children are on the team.

3.     My brother runs every day. He runs at the track. My brother is six years old. He can run very fast.

4.     Sam plays football. He kicks the football. Sam kicks the football very far. Tomorrow is Saturday.

5.     Allison likes to play kick ball. It is time for lunch. She plays kick ball with her friends. They play after school.

## *Apply*

**C.** Think of a sentence to finish the paragraph. Keep to the main idea. Write the paragraph.

6.     Yesterday Hope won a jumping contest. She jumped very far.

# LANGUAGE REVIEW

**Understanding Paragraphs**    pages 120–121

Read each paragraph and the choices below it.
Write the main idea.

1.    Mark and Yoko had fun at the beach. Yoko built a sand castle. Mark looked for shells and stones. Then they ran into the ocean.
      **a.** looking for shells
      **b.** having fun at the beach

2.    The family enjoyed eating lunch at the beach. Everyone ate chicken. They also drank orange juice. For dessert they had watermelon.
      **a.** eating lunch at the beach
      **b.** eating chicken

**Beginning Paragraphs**    pages 122–123

Copy the paragraphs. Underline each sentence that tells the main idea.

3.    My cat likes to hide from me. It hides behind doors. My cat even hides in closets. Then it waits for me to find it.

**4.** My class has a pet hamster. The hamster lives in a cage. It is brown and white. The hamster eats sunflower seeds.

## Keeping to the Main Idea    pages 124–125

Read each paragraph. Write the sentence that does not tell about the main idea.

**5.** Sabrina and Betty are friends. They walk to school together. Sabrina and Betty eat lunch together. Today is Wednesday. They also play baseball after school.

**6.** Ellis is a busy person. He works hard in school. After school he delivers newspapers. At night Ellis helps cook dinner. Ellis has brown hair.

## Applying Paragraphs

Think of a sentence to finish the paragraph. Keep to the main idea. Write the paragraph.

**7.** Everyone looks different. Some people have long hair. Others have short hair. Some people are tall.

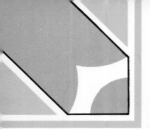

# STUDY SKILLS

## Lesson 4: Understanding Antonyms

Meg and Peg are twins. Look at the picture. Name one way they are alike. Name one way they are different.

### Think and Discuss

Meg and Peg are the same in some ways. In many ways they are exactly opposite.

When Meg feels happy, Peg feels the opposite. She feels sad. The word <u>sad</u> is the **antonym** of <u>happy</u>. When Meg is <u>cold</u>, what is Peg? Tell why.

> ● **Antonyms** are words with opposite meanings.

### Practice

**A.** Copy each numbered word. Find its antonym in the box on the next page. Write each antonym next to the word.

**1.** tall     **2.** dry     **3.** heavy

**4.** thick     **5.** different     **6.** empty

**128**   VOCABULARY: Antonyms

| same | short | light |
|------|-------|-------|
| thin | full | wet |

**B.** Copy the sentences. Underline the antonyms.

7. As Meg climbs up, Peg climbs down.
8. Meg feels hungry. Peg feels full.
9. Meg is inside. Peg is outside.
10. When Meg goes north, Peg goes south.
11. When Meg gets to school early, Peg is late.

**C.** Read each sentence about Peg. Notice the underlined word. Choose an antonym for it to complete each sentence about Meg. Choose from the two words in ( ). Write the complete sentence about Meg.

12. Peg is <u>asleep</u>.
    Meg is _____. (awake, found)
13. Peg likes the <u>country</u>.
    Meg likes the _____. (city, noise)
14. Peg uses her <u>right</u> hand.
    Meg uses her _____ hand. (strong, left)

## Apply

**D. 15.–18.** Write two pairs of sentences about the twins. Use words that are antonyms in your sentences.

# Lesson 5: Understanding Words That Sound the Same

Read the sentences. Note the underlined words.

1. <u>Eight</u> ducks walked by me.
2. One duck <u>ate</u> my lunch!

## Think and Discuss

Say the underlined words. <u>Eight</u> and <u>ate</u> sound the same. Think about how the words are different. How is each word spelled? What does <u>eight</u> mean? What does <u>ate</u> mean?

Some words sound the same. They have different spellings. They also have different meanings.

## Practice

**A.** Write each numbered word. Next to it write a word from the box. The word must sound the same. It must have a different spelling and meaning.

**1.** I     **2.** write     **3.** our
**4.** one     **5.** here     **6.** too

| | | | | | |
|---|---|---|---|---|---|
| right | won | eye | two | hear | hour |

**B. 7.–12.** Listen as your teacher reads some directions.

**C.** Write the sentence pairs. Underline the two words that sound the same.

**13.** Did you see it?     I saw the sea.
**14.** The house is red.     I read a story.
**15.** Is the sail fixed?     Tomatoes are on sale.
**16.** What would you like?     I want some wood.

## Apply

**D.** Choose the correct word in (   ) to complete each sentence. Write the sentences.

**17.** The dog dug a (hole, whole).
**18.** Let's go (to, two) the store.
**19.** We cooked the (meet, meat).
**20.** Carol is (won, one) year old.

## A Challenge

There are ten mistakes in the paragraph. Find them. Write the paragraph correctly.

The whether was cold last knight. The wind blue hard. Eye looked out the window. Their were for dear in the yard. First they eight hour flours. Then they nibbled part of the bushes.

# Lesson 6: Building Words with Prefixes

Read the sentences.

1. The cat is <u>afraid</u> of the dog.
2. The dog is <u>unafraid</u> of the cat.

Which animal is afraid? Which animal is not afraid?

## Think and Discuss

Do <u>afraid</u> and <u>unafraid</u> have the same meaning? You can change a word's meaning by adding letters to the beginning of it. The letters <u>un</u> were added to the beginning of <u>afraid</u>. Letters added to the beginning of a word are a **prefix.**

<u>Un</u> is a prefix. The prefix <u>un</u> means "not." The word <u>unafraid</u> means "not afraid."

Now read these sentences.

3. Please <u>fill</u> the dog's bowl.
4. Now <u>refill</u> the cat's bowl.

Look at the underlined words. Which word has a prefix? Use this chart to find the meaning of the prefix.

| Prefix | Meaning | Example |
|--------|---------|---------|
| un | not | unlucky |
| re | again | redo |

> ● A **prefix** is a group of letters added
> to the beginning of a word.

## *Practice*

**A.** Copy the sentences. Underline each
word that has a prefix.

1. The deer is unhurt.
2. Tim rewrote the letter.
3. Are you unhappy?
4. The directions are unclear.
5. Fran repainted the wagon.
6. Did you rewrap the present?

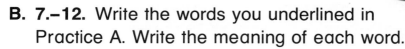

**B. 7.–12.** Write the words you underlined in
Practice A. Write the meaning of each word.

## *Apply*

**C.** Write a sentence for each word.

| | | |
|---|---|---|
| **13.** cover | **14.** uncover | **15.** snapped |
| **16.** unsnapped | **17.** heat | **18.** reheat |

### *To Memorize*

The only way to have a friend is to be one.

Ralph Waldo Emerson

Would you want to be <u>your</u> friend? Why?

# Lesson 7: Building Words with Suffixes

Reuse is a word with a prefix. The prefix re was added to use. The prefix changes the meaning of use. Reuse means "use again."

Letters can be added to the end of use too. Read the sentences.

1. The large plate is useful.
2. A broken glass is useless.

## Think and Discuss

Letters added to the end of a word are a **suffix.** A suffix changes a word's meaning.

Read sentence 1 again. Useful is a word with a suffix. What letters were added to use? The suffix ful means "full of." Useful means "full of use."

The suffix less means "without." Read sentence 2. What does useless mean?

Read this sentence.

3. The glass is breakable.

Which word has a suffix? Use the chart on the next page to find the meaning of the suffix.

| Suffix | Meaning | Example |
|--------|---------|---------|
| ful | full of | hopeful |
| less | without | harmless |
| able | able to be | wearable |

 ● A **suffix** is a group of letters added to the end of a word.

# Practice

**A.** Copy the sentences. Underline each word that has a suffix.

1. The plate is colorful.
2. Is the towel washable?
3. The water is soapless.
4. A cook should be careful.
5. The kitchen is spotless.
6. Is my recipe readable?

**B. 7.–12.** Write the words you underlined in Practice A. Next to each word write its meaning.

# Apply

**C.** Write a sentence for each word.

**13.** thankful      **14.** fearless
**15.** drinkable     **16.** playful
**17.** harmless      **18.** trainable

# COMPOSITION

## *Lesson 8: Writing a Story Beginning*

Talk about the picture.

### Think and Discuss

Ted is writing a story about the picture. Read the story beginning.

> Last Saturday my friends and I went to the playground. The playground was very dirty.

A story beginning tells about the people in a story. Who are the people in this story? A story beginning tells where a story takes place. Where does this story take place?

### Practice

**A.** Read each story beginning. <u>Who</u> are the people in each story? Write their names. Write <u>where</u> the story takes place.

1.    A funny thing happened yesterday. Sam and Cindy were at the zoo.

**2.** Elvin is home from school. He is sick.

**3.** Yesterday it snowed. Gillian went skating at the pond.

**B.** Finish each story beginning. Name the people in the story. Write each story beginning.

**4.** A funny thing happened yesterday. _____ were at the zoo.

**5.** Yesterday it snowed. _____ went skating at the pond.

**6.** _____ is a pet dog. _____ is lost at the park.

**C.** Finish each story beginning. Tell <u>where</u> the story takes place. Write each story beginning.

**7.** A funny thing happened yesterday. Sam and Cindy were at the _____.

**8.** Fran went on vacation. She visited _____.

**9.** Buffy is a pet dog. Buffy is lost in the _____.

## Apply

**D. 10.** Write a story beginning. Use one of these ideas. Tell <u>who</u> is in the story. Tell <u>where</u> the story takes place.

> winning a contest
> having a party
> finding a magic stone

# Lesson 9: Writing the Middle of a Story

Here is the story Ted has written so far.

Last Saturday my friends and I went to the playground. The playground was very dirty.

Now Ted is going to write the middle of the story.

## Think and Discuss

The middle of a story is the main part of the story. It tells what the characters do. Read the middle of Ted's story.

We could not play there. Felicia and I picked up the garbage. Then Kim painted a sign. The sign said, "Please keep our playground clean."

The children wanted a clean playground. What did the children do first? What did they do next? Sentences in a story must be in order. Then the story will make sense.

# Practice

**A.** Each group of sentences tells the main part of a story. The sentences are not in order. Write them in order.

1. **a.** Mother lit some candles.
   **b.** The lights went out.
   **c.** A terrible storm began.

2. **a.** The moving van came.
   **b.** The workers carried out the furniture.
   **c.** They put the furniture into the van.

3. **a.** The plane left Miami.
   **b.** Then the plane landed in Houston.
   **c.** Susan ate dinner on the plane.

# Apply

**B. 4.** Look at the story beginning you wrote in Lesson 8. Write a main part for your story. Tell what the characters do. Be sure your sentences are in order. Do not end the story.

# Lesson 10: Writing a Story Ending

Talk about the picture. This is how Ted's story ends.

Please keep our playground clean.

## Think and Discuss

Read the beginning and middle of Ted's story.

Last Saturday my friends and I went to the playground. The playground was very dirty. We could not play there. Felicia and I picked up the garbage. Then Kim painted a sign. The sign said, "Please keep our playground clean."

The ending of a story tells how things worked out. It finishes the story. Which is the better ending for Ted's story?

1. Now we play in a clean playground.
2. The sign looks nice.

## Practice

**A.** Copy each story. Then choose the best ending. Add it to your story.

1.   My father took me to the park. He gave me money for a pony ride. A girl led the pony around the park. Then she let me ride alone.

   **a.** It was a cold day.
   **b.** Father does not like ponies.
   **c.** I had fun at the park.

2.   My dog Casper was lost. I looked for Casper in the house. Then Mother and I drove around the neighborhood. We saw a dog.

   **a.** Casper is a good dog.
   **b.** It was Casper.
   **c.** I was hungry.

## Apply

**B. 3.** Read the story you wrote in Lessons 8 and 9. Write an ending for it. Tell how things worked out in the story.

# Lesson 11: Writing a Story

Carol wrote a story about a funny pig. Read the story.

> The Jogging Pig
>     Penjy was a funny pig who lived on a farm. Penjy liked to jog. He jogged all around the farm. Then there was a big race. Guess who won? Penjy won the race.

## Think and Discuss

Does Carol's story have a beginning? Does it have a middle and an end? Who is the story about? Where does the story take place?

Carol's story has a **title.** The title is "The Jogging Pig." A title gives a hint about the story. Which words in the title begin with a capital letter? When you write a title, begin the first word with a capital letter. Begin all important words with a capital letter too.

Look at the story again. How many paragraphs do you see? Every story has at least one paragraph. The first line of each paragraph is **indented.**

**How to Write a Story**

1. **Write a beginning. Tell who the story is about. Tell where the story takes place.**
2. **Write the main part. Tell what the characters do. Tell what happens in order.**
3. **Write an ending. Tell how things work out.**
4. **Give the story a title. Begin the first word and all important words with capital letters.**

## *Practice*

**A.** Think about a funny animal. Plan a story about it. Write the answers to these questions.

1. Who is in your story?
2. Where does the story take place?
3. What do the characters do?
4. How does the story end?

## *Apply*

**B. 5.** Look at your answers for Practice A. Use the answers to write a story. Check your story. Does it have a beginning, a middle, and an end? Does your story have a title?

# Lesson 12: Editing a Story

Mario wrote a story. Then he edited it carefully. He read it to find mistakes. He also wanted to see if he could make the story better. Read the story.

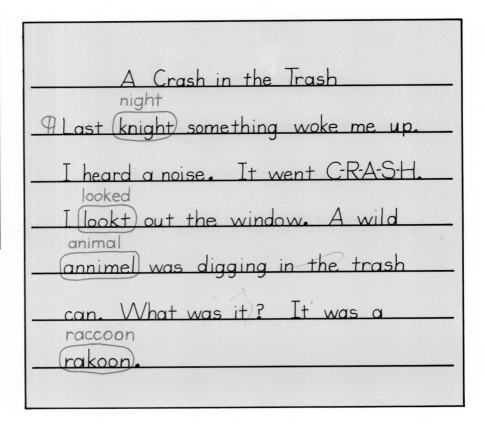

A Crash in the Trash

Last (knight) something woke me up. *night*

I heard a noise. It went C-R-A-S-H.

I (lookt) out the window. A wild *looked*

(annimel) was digging in the trash *animal*

can. What was it? It was a

(rakoon). *raccoon*

## Think and Discuss

Look at the beginning of the story. Mario used this editing mark ᖰ. It means you should indent for a paragraph. Why did Mario use this editing mark? Mario also made four other changes. He used this editing mark ○. Why did Mario circle the words? What did he write above them?

## Practice

**A.** Rewrite Mario's story. Make all the changes he made.

## Apply

**B.** Read the story you wrote in Lesson 11. Edit it. Then write the story correctly.

---

# MECHANICS PRACTICE

### Writing Paragraphs

● The first line of a paragraph is indented.

Write each paragraph correctly.

1. Ben and Sandy are baking cookies. The cookies are in the oven. They must bake for ten minutes.
2. Father cooked dinner yesterday. He made stew. He also made carrots and potatoes. The dinner was very good.

# LITERATURE

## Lesson 13: Reading a Tale

Read the story.

### Little Tuppen

by Paul Galdone

Once upon a time, an old hen whose name was Cluck-cluck and her little chick Tuppen went into the woods. They were busy all day scratching among the leaves finding seeds to eat.

"Be careful," said Cluck-cluck. "Eat only the smaller seeds. The big ones may make you cough."

After a while Little Tuppen tried to eat a big seed. Then he began to cough. Cluck-cluck in great fright ran to fetch him some water.

She ran to the spring and said, "Dear spring, please give me some water. Little Tuppen is coughing."

"I will give you some water if you will bring me a cup," the spring said.

Cluck-cluck ran to the oak tree. Then she said, "Dear oak tree, please give me a cup. Then the spring will give me some water. Little Tuppen is coughing."

The oak tree liked Tuppen and wanted to help. It said, "I will give you a cup if someone will shake my branches."

So Cluck-cluck ran to the woodcutter's little boy. "Dear little boy, please shake the oak tree's branches," she said. "Then the oak tree will give me a cup, and the spring will give me some water. Little Tuppen is coughing."

The little boy said, "If you give me some shoes, I will shake the oak tree's branches."

Cluck-cluck ran to the shoemaker and said, "Dear shoemaker, please give me some shoes for the little boy. Then the little boy will shake the oak tree's branches and the oak tree will give me a cup. Then the

spring will give me some water. Little Tuppen is coughing."

The shoemaker said, "Give me some leather. Then I will make some shoes for the little boy."

Cluck-cluck knew the cow had some leather. She ran to the cow and said, "Dear cow, please give me some leather. Then the shoemaker will make shoes for the little boy. The little boy will shake the oak tree's branches. The oak tree will give me a cup and the spring will give me some water. Little Tuppen is coughing."

"I will give you some leather if you will give me some corn," the cow said.

So Cluck-cluck ran to the farmer and said, "Dear farmer, please give me some corn for the cow. Then the cow will give me some leather for the shoemaker, and the shoemaker will make shoes for the little boy. Then the little boy will shake the oak tree's branches, and the oak tree will give me a cup. Then the spring will give me some water. Little Tuppen is coughing."

The farmer said, "I need a plow before I can give you some corn."

Then Cluck-cluck ran to the blacksmith and said, "Dear blacksmith, please give me a plow for the farmer. Then the farmer will give me some corn for the cow. When the cow gets the corn it will give me some leather for the shoemaker. Then the shoemaker will give me some shoes for the little boy and the little boy will shake the oak tree's branches. The oak tree will give me a cup and the spring will give me some water. Little Tuppen is coughing."

The blacksmith said to Cluck-cluck, "I will give you a plow if you will give me some iron."

Cluck-cluck had heard about some elves who lived under the mountains. The elves had a lot of iron. She told the elves about Little Tuppen and the big seed.

The elves wanted to help. So they brought out a heap of iron for the blacksmith.

Cluck-cluck brought the iron to the blacksmith. He made a plow for the farmer. The farmer gave some corn for the cow. The

cow gave some leather for the shoemaker. Then the shoemaker made some shoes for the little boy. When the little boy got the shoes he shook the oak tree's branches. Then the oak tree gave Cluck-cluck a cup, and the spring gave some water. Cluck-cluck gave the water to Little Tuppen.

Little Tuppen drank the water and stopped coughing. He ran chirping and scratching among the leaves as if nothing had happened.

## Think and Discuss

"Little Tuppen" is a very old story. A very old story is called a **tale.** Magical things sometimes happen in a tale. What is magical in this tale?

Name everyone in the tale who helped Cluck-cluck. Everyone who helped is called a **character.** Cluck-cluck and Tuppen are characters too. Where does the story take place? The **setting** of a story is where it takes place. A story may have more than one setting.

## Practice

**A.** Answer the questions.

1. Where were Cluck-cluck and Tuppen looking for seeds? Write the name of the place.
2. Which character tried to eat a big seed? Write the name of the character.
3. Which character did Cluck-cluck run to first? Write the name of the character.
4. Which character did Cluck-cluck run to for corn? Write the name of the character.
5. Where did the elves live? Write the name of the place.

## Apply

**B. 6.** Pick a story from your reader. Write the characters in the story. Write the setting.

## A BOOK TO READ

Title: **The Book of Giant Stories**
Author: David L. Harrison
Publisher: American Heritage Press

The three stories in this book tell about giants. A boy tells or teaches a giant something in each story. What could a boy teach a giant? Read the stories to find out.

# 5 UNIT TEST

● **Understanding Paragraphs**   pages 120–125

Read the paragraph. Answer the questions.
Write the correct letter.

Dogs can do many tricks. Some dogs can roll over. Other dogs beg for treats. My dog is brown and white. Still other dogs can catch a ball.

1. What is the main idea of the paragraph?
   a. Dogs can do many tricks.
   b. Dogs can run fast.
2. The first line of the paragraph is _____.
   a. too long
   b. indented
3. Which sentence does not tell about the main idea?
   a. My dog is brown and white.
   b. Some dogs can roll over.

● **Understanding Antonyms**   pages 128–129

Copy each numbered word. Find its antonym in the box.
Write each antonym.

1. under    2. in    3. wet    4. slow

| fast    over    out    dry |
|---|

## ● Understanding Words That Sound the Same    pages 130–131

Choose the correct word in ( ) to complete each sentence. Write each sentence.

5. Did you (see, sea) Mike?
6. (To, Two) birds flew by.
7. I like to (write, right) letters.
8. Please come over (hear, here).
9. My baseball team (won, one) the game.

## ● Prefixes and Suffixes    pages 132–135

Copy the sentences. Underline each word that has a prefix or a suffix.

10. Dan is very unhappy.
11. The classroom is spotless.
12. Please rewrap the box.
13. The puppy is very playful.
14. Did you uncover the pot?
15. Which shirt is washable?

## ● Writing and Editing a Story    pages 136–145

Write a story. Tell about a time you helped someone. Edit your story.

## ● Reading a Tale    pages 146–151

Answer the questions.

1. What is a tale?
2. What are the people in a tale called?
3. What is the place where a tale happens called?

# LANGUAGE
## Learning About Describing Words

# STUDY SKILLS
## Finding Information

# COMPOSITION
## Writing Paragraphs and Reports

# LITERATURE
## Reading a Play

Look at the pictures. What do you see? Pick one thing to talk about. Tell about its size, shape, and color. Use words that <u>describe</u> what you are seeing.

Choose a boy or girl in one of the pictures. How do you think that boy or girl feels? What are some other words that name feelings? Words like <u>happy</u> and <u>excited</u> are describing words too.

Play a game with your class. Find something in your classroom to describe. Do not tell its name. Choose words that tell how the object feels, smells, or sounds. Let your friends guess the object you are describing.

# LANGUAGE

## Lesson 1: Understanding Describing Words

Look at the picture. Then answer the questions.

What <u>color</u> is block 1? What <u>size</u> is block 2? What <u>shape</u> is block 3?

### *Think and Discuss*

The word <u>block</u> is a noun. Words such as <u>red</u>, <u>large</u>, and <u>round</u> tell about the noun. They **describe** the noun. Words that describe nouns are called **describing words.** Describing words can tell about color, size, or shape. They can tell how something feels or tastes. They can tell how something sounds or smells.

Now read these sentences.

1. I made a large <u>castle</u> with red <u>blocks</u>.
2. The square <u>blocks</u> fell with a loud <u>noise</u>.
3. The sticky <u>paste</u> has a strange <u>smell</u>.

The underlined words are nouns. Find the word that describes each noun.

> ● A **describing word** is a word that describes a noun.

# Practice

**A.** Write the word that describes each underlined noun.

1. We built a little <u>town</u> out of blocks.
2. The trees were made of green <u>paper</u>.
3. A thin <u>road</u> was made of pebbles.
4. One house had tiny <u>windows</u>.
5. I put them on with smooth <u>tape</u>.

**B.** Copy each sentence. Underline the noun. Circle the describing word that tells about each noun.

6. I like building with square blocks.
7. Where did the yellow block go?
8. The big tree fell down.
9. I used gray clay to hold it up.
10. It has a terrible smell.

# Apply

**C.** Write five sentences about this picture. Use the describing words below.

11. green  12. short  13. blue  14. thin  15. square

# Lesson 2: Describing Feelings

Look at the faces. Faces can tell about feelings. Think about how each person feels.

## Think and Discuss

Words can tell about feelings too. **Describing words** can describe feelings. The man in the picture looks happy. Happy is a describing word. It describes how the man feels.

Now read these sentences.

1. Carmen is surprised.
2. Mrs. Zack is glad.
3. Luke seems frightened.
4. The baby is unhappy.

The underlined words are nouns. Which word describes how Carmen feels? Which word describes how Mrs. Zack feels? What is the describing word in sentence 3? What is the describing word in sentence 4?

Some describing words tell how things look. Others tell about feelings.

## Practice

**A.** Write the words that describe feelings.

1. Ray feels happy.        2. Jeff is excited.
3. That girl is angry.     4. Dena is pleased.
5. The shy boy sat down.   6. The sad baby cried.

**B.** Look at the pictures. How does each person feel? Think of a describing word to finish each sentence. Write the sentences.

**7.** Gena feels _____.

**8.** Mr. Chu is _____.

## *Apply*

**C. 9.–12.** Write four sentences about playing a game. Use describing words. Tell how you feel when you play the game.

## HOW OUR LANGUAGE GROWS

To tell what something is like, we sometimes name a part of the body. A clock has a face. A plane has a nose. Telling about things this way helps to describe them.

**1.** Answer each riddle. Write the correct word.

    **a.** I have two hands but cannot feel.      | chair
    **b.** I have many teeth but cannot chew.  | clock
    **c.** I have long arms but cannot reach.   | comb

**2.** Make up a riddle of your own. Pick one of these body parts.

        leg    foot    head    mouth    eye

# Lesson 3: Describing How Many

This is Fizz. He is from the land of Zizz. How many heads does Fizz have?

## Think and Discuss

**Describing words** can tell <u>how</u> <u>many</u>. Fizz has three eyes. <u>Three</u> is a describing word. It tells how many eyes Fizz has.

Read these sentences. Find the describing words.

1. Fizz has <u>four</u> arms.
2. There are <u>many</u> monsters just like Fizz.

The underlined words are describing words. Can you tell exactly how many monsters are just like Fizz? Words like <u>some</u>, <u>several</u>, and <u>many</u> do not tell exact numbers. They still describe how many.

Find the describing words in these sentences.

3. Fizz has visited many places.
4. He met some monsters and twenty people.

Describing words can tell about color, shape, or size. They can tell about feelings. They can tell how many.

## Practice

**A.** Study these sentences. Then close your book. Write the sentences as your teacher reads them. Remember to begin and end your sentences correctly.

1. I have one head.
2. You have two ears.
3. Bugs have many feet.
4. Birds have two eyes.
5. Do frogs have ten toes?
6. Some frogs look funny.

**B.** Copy the sentences. Underline the describing words.

7. Fizz has seven brothers.
8. Many monsters live in the land of Zizz.
9. Fizz owns several boats and one plane.

**C.** Think of describing words to finish each sentence. Write the sentences.

10. My monster has _____ eyes.
11. It walks on its _____ feet.

## Apply

**D. 12.–15.** Draw your own monster. Write four sentences about it. Use four different words that tell how many.

# Lesson 4: Comparing Things

Look at the pictures. Read the sentences.

1. The first bug is <u>small</u>.
2. The second bug is <u>smaller</u> than the first bug.
3. The third bug is the <u>smallest</u> bug of the three.

## Think and Discuss

The underlined words describe the noun <u>bug</u>. **Describing words** can be used to **compare** things. When two things are compared, add <u>er</u> to most describing words. Which underlined word is used to compare two things? What two things are being compared?

Add <u>est</u> to most describing words when more than two things are being compared. Which underlined word is used to compare more than two things? What things are being compared?

Compare these two butterflies. Which one is smaller?

Compare these spiders. Which one is smallest?

- Add <u>er</u> to most describing words when they are used to compare two things.
- Add <u>est</u> to most describing words when they are used to compare more than two things.

## Practice

**A.** Copy this chart. Fill in the correct describing words.

| | | |
|---|---|---|
| **1.** small | smaller | smallest |
| **2.** tall | _____ | tallest |
| **3.** short | shorter | _____ |
| **4.** _____ | faster | fastest |

**B.** Choose the correct word. Write the sentences.

**5.** This ant is (slow, slower) than that one.

**6.** This spider is the (small, smallest) of the three.

**7.** One bug climbed the (taller, tallest) plant in the garden.

**8.** The worm is (longer, longest) than the spider.

## Apply

**C.** Use these four describing words in sentences. You may compare things that you see around you.

**9.** thicker   **10.** thickest

**11.** shorter   **12.** shortest

# LANGUAGE REVIEW

## Describing Words    pages 156–157

Copy the sentences. Underline the describing words.

1. The small boy ran away.
2. A brown dog chased him.
3. They saw a square box.
4. A sweet smell came from it.
5. The dog gave a loud bark.
6. A large fish was in the box.
7. The boy opened the big box.
8. He picked up the white fish.
9. The fish had smooth scales.
10. The dog ate the fat fish.

## Words That Describe Feelings    pages 158–159

Pick the words from the box that describe feelings.
Use those words to write the sentences below.

| | | | |
|---|---|---|---|
| angry | red | sad | round |
| deep | thin | proud | big |
| happy | long | salty | three |

11. Ann was _____ when her dog ran away.
12. She was _____ when it came back.
13. She was _____ when it chased a car.
14. She was _____ when it won a prize.

## Words That Tell How Many    pages 160–161

Look at the pictures. Write the word in (   ) that tells how many.

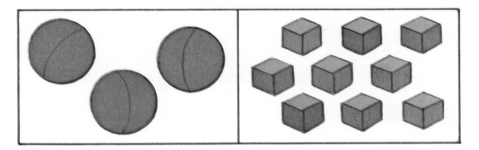

**15.** (three, red)        **16.** (square, nine)

## Comparisons    pages 162–163

Choose the correct word in (   ). Write the sentences.

**17.** Mary is (tall, taller) than Juan.
**18.** Juan is (shorter, shortest) than Mary.
**19.** Mary is the (taller, tallest) girl in our class.
**20.** Dan is the (taller, tallest) boy I know.
**21.** Is Dan (smaller, smallest) than Mary?

## Applying Describing Words

Read the riddle. Then follow the directions.

I am white and wet. I fall in winter.
What am I? (snow)

Use describing words. Write a riddle about each of these things.

**22.** a chair    **23.** a food    **24.** an animal

## Lesson 5: Using the Library

Read the poem with your class. Name some books you have found in the library.

### At the Library

This is a lovely place to be.
    The books are everywhere.
And I can read them here, or take
    Them home and read them there.

Marchette Chute

## Think and Discuss

Some books are called **fiction.** They are stories about pretend people and things. Curious George is fiction. It is about a make-believe monkey.

**Nonfiction** books tell about real people or things. Big Tracks, Little Tracks is nonfiction. It gives facts about animal tracks.

A library has fiction and nonfiction books. The fiction books are on some shelves. The nonfiction are on other shelves. Where would you find a book on growing plants? Where would a book called The Purple Cow be?

## Practice

**A.** Where would you find these books? Write
<u>fiction</u> or <u>nonfiction</u>.

1. a book about how sharks get food
2. a book about a magic carpet
3. a book about an elf
4. a book about training puppies
5. a book about a talking horse

## Apply

**B. 6.** Look in your library. Find one fiction book.
Find one nonfiction book. Share them with your
class. You might like to read the books and
talk about them.

**To Memorize**

The library is my favorite place,
I go there every day;
I put my nose into a book,
And then I fly away . . .

Lois Lenski

What does the poet mean when she says, "I fly
away"? What kinds of books can make <u>you</u> fly
away? Tell why.

# Lesson 6: Using Parts of a Book

Some parts of a book are helpful to a reader. Look at these pictures. They show pages from a book.

TITLE PAGE

Facts About Reptiles

by
Lauren Foster

TABLE OF CONTENTS

1. What Are
   Reptiles? . . . . . . . .   1
2. Dinosaurs . . . . . . .  11
3. Snakes . . . . . . . . .  20
4. Lizards . . . . . . . . .  32
5. Crocodiles . . . . . .  43
6. Turtles . . . . . . . . .  51

INDEX

Age of Reptiles, 12
Alligator, 46
Asian snakes, 27–30
Brontosaurus, 8–10
Chameleon, 34
Climate, 21, 54
Cold-blooded,
   defined, 2

## Think and Discuss

The **title** is the name of the book. The **author** is the person who wrote the book. Which page lists the title and author of this book?

Some books have a **table of contents.** This lists the chapters or parts of a book. It tells the page number where each chapter begins. This book has six chapters. On what page does chapter 4 begin?

Many nonfiction books have an **index.** An index is in ABC order. It lists many things that can be found in the book. It tells the page numbers where these things can be found. Look at the index on page 168. On what page could you find facts about an alligator?

## Practice

A. Look at the pages pictured on page 168. Answer these questions.

1. Is the author named Lauren Foster?
2. Does chapter 3 begin on page 32?
3. Are there facts about climate on page 54?
4. Which page lists the title and author?
5. Which page lists chapter names?

## Apply

B. Find the table of contents in this book. Look at the names of the units, or chapters.

6. On what page does Unit 2 begin?
7. On what page does Unit 6 begin?

## A Challenge

Look in your library. Find a nonfiction book that has a table of contents. Find a nonfiction book that has an index. Share the books with your class.

# Lesson 7: Using a Map

Norma wants to go to Jan's house. She looks at a **map** to find out how to get there.

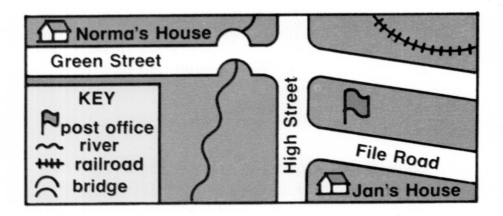

## Think and Discuss

A map is a picture of a place. Most maps have a **key.** A key explains the marks used on the map.

Look at the key on Norma's map. What does this mark ⌒ mean? Point to the river on the map.

## Practice

**A.** Answer these questions. Write <u>yes</u> or <u>no</u>.

1. Does the railroad cross Green Street?
2. Will Norma have to cross a bridge?
3. Will she have to cross High Street?

## Apply

**B. 4.** Draw a map that shows part of your classroom. Make a key on your map.

# *Lesson 8: Taking Notes*

Chan read this paragraph about dolphins.

A dolphin is a fast and graceful swimmer. It is a mammal that lives in the ocean. Usually dolphins live in groups called schools.

## *Think and Discuss*

Chan took **notes** on the paragraph he read. Notes are short sentences that help you remember what you read. Tell only important facts when you take notes. Write them in your own words.

Read Chan's notes. Did he write all the important facts? Did he use his own words?

> Dolphins are good swimmers.
> They are mammals.
> They live in schools.

## *Practice*

**A.** Take notes on this paragraph.

A sick or hurt dolphin gets help fast. Other dolphins swim right alongside it. They push it to the surface to breathe.

## *Apply*

**B.** Find a paragraph in a nonfiction book. Take notes on the paragraph.

# COMPOSITION

## Lesson 9: Combining Sentences

Read these sentences.

1. The runners lined up.
2. The runners waited.
3. The runners lined up <u>and</u> waited.

What is the noun in all three sentences?

### Think and Discuss

The nouns are the same in sentences 1 and 2. Two sentences that tell about the same noun can be combined. The word <u>and</u> is used to join them.

### Practice

**A.** Do these sentence pairs tell about the same noun? Write <u>yes</u> or <u>no</u>.

1. Runners move quickly. Runners race by.
2. Terry runs fast. One girl cheers.
3. People call to him. People clap.

### Apply

**B.** Join this sentence. Use the word <u>and</u>.

4. People watch. People cheer.

# Lesson 10: Writing a How-to Paragraph

Nick wrote a paragraph. Read what he wrote.

> I set the table every night. First I put out the plates. Then I fold the napkins. Last I put out forks and knives.

## Think and Discuss

Nick told his readers how to do something. He told about it in order. His first sentence tells what the paragraph is about. The underlined words help his readers understand the order. What did Nick do first? What did he do last?

## Practice

**A.** Write this paragraph in correct order.

We clean up the art room. Next we cover the paint jars. Last we throw away papers. First we clean the brushes.

## Apply

**B.** Write a how-to paragraph. Use one of these ideas.

How to Water a Plant    How to Wash a Window
How to Feed a Dog       How to Play Tag

# Lesson 11: Writing a Book Report

Julie wanted to share a book she liked. One way to share a book is to tell about it in a **book report.** Read Julie's book report.

---

**Title**  Gus and Buster Work Things Out

**Author**  Andrew Bronin

**About the Book**  This book is about Gus and Buster. They are brothers who do not always get along. Gus tries to teach Buster good manners.

**What I Think**  This book made me laugh. People who like funny stories will like this book.

---

## Think and Discuss

What is the title of Julie's book? Notice that most words in the title begin with capital letters. Always begin the first word, the last word, and all important words in a title with capital letters. Always underline the title of a book.

Julie also told the author's name. Then she told some interesting facts about the book. What did she tell about last?

> **How to Write a Book Report**
>
> 1. **Write the title of the book.**
> 2. **Write the author's name.**
> 3. **Tell some facts about the book.**
> 4. **Tell what you think about the book.**

## Practice

**A.** Read this book report. Then answer the questions below.

**Title** Dorothy Hamill

**Author** S.H. Burchard

**About the Book** This book is about a famous skater. Her name is Dorothy Hamill. She wanted to be the United States champion. She worked very hard. In 1974 she had her big chance.

**What I Think** This book is exciting. I learned many things about skaters.

1. What is the title of this book? Write it correctly.
2. What is the author's name?
3. What is this book about?

## Apply

**B. 4.** Write a book report about a book you read.

= capitalize

⊙ make a period

∧ add something

∧, add a comma

⌐ take something away

◯ spell correctly

¶ indent the paragraph

# Lesson 12: Editing a Book Report

Jess wrote a report about her favorite book. Then she corrected some mistakes in her report. Read the report.

---

**Title** The climb

**Author** carol carrick

**About the Book** Brendan and Nora
                                                 tall
climb a ∧ mountain. Nora tries to scare
                                    dark
Brendan. She hides in a ∧ cave. Then

she gets stuck.

**What I Think** This book is exciting. I
            beautiful
like the ∧ pictures.

---

## Think and Discuss

Jess used editing marks to make changes in her book report. This mark ∧ means to add something. What words did Jess add to her report? She used one other editing mark. What is it? What does that mark mean? Why did Jess use the mark in her report?

## Practice

**A.** Write Jess's book report correctly.

## Apply

**B.** Look at the book report you wrote in Lesson 11. Did you use capital letters correctly? Did you begin and end each sentence correctly? Could you add any describing words to make your report more interesting? Edit your report. Then write it correctly.

## MECHANICS PRACTICE

### Writing Book Titles

● Begin the first word, last word, and all important words in a title with a capital letter.
● Underline the title of a book.

Write these book titles correctly.

1. george and martha
2. alligators all around
3. on beyond zebra
4. the amazing pig
5. three funny ducks
6. the world of rockets
7. train ride
8. the sorely trying day
9. our national parks
10. how to draw horses

# LITERATURE

## *Lesson 13: Reading a Play*

A play is one way of telling a story. Listen as your teacher reads this play.

### The Mouse and the Winds

by Arnold Lobel

Characters:

| | | |
|---|---|---|
| **Storyteller** | **Mouse** | **West Wind** |
| **House** | **East Wind** | **Tree** |
| **South Wind** | **Mountain** | **North Wind** |
| **Lake** | **Island** | **Lady** |

**Storyteller:** A mouse went out in his boat, but there was no wind. The boat did not move.

**Mouse:** Wind! Come down and blow my boat across this lake!

**West Wind:** Here I am.

**Storyteller:** The west wind blew and blew. The mouse and the boat went up in the air — and landed on the roof of a house.

**House:** Ouch!

| | |
|---|---|
| **Mouse:** | Wind! Come down and blow my boat off this house! |
| **East Wind:** | Here I am. |
| **Storyteller:** | The east wind blew and blew. The mouse and the boat and the house went up in the air — and landed on the top of a tree. |
| **Tree:** | Hey! |
| **Mouse:** | Wind! Come down and blow my boat off this house and off this tree! |
| **South Wind:** | Here I am. |
| **Storyteller:** | The south wind blew and blew. The mouse and the boat and the house and the tree went up in the air — and landed on the top of a mountain. |
| **Mountain:** | What's going on? |
| **Mouse:** | Wind! Come down and blow my boat off this house and off this tree and off this mountain. |
| **North Wind:** | Here I am. |
| **Storyteller:** | The north wind blew and blew. The mouse and the boat and the house and the tree and the mountain went up in |

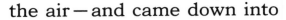

the air — and came down into the lake.

**Lake:** Splash!

**Storyteller:** The mountain sank and became an island.

**Island:** Hi there.

**Storyteller:** The house landed next to the tree.

**House:** Excuse me.

**Storyteller:** A lady looked out of a window in the house and said:

**Lady:** What a nice place to live!

**Storyteller:** And the mouse just sailed away.

**Mouse:** So long.

## Think and Discuss

A play has **characters,** just as a story does. A play is supposed to be read aloud. It is supposed to be acted out. People act out the parts of each character. They are called **actors.**

This play has one character who does not act. **Storyteller** just tells the story.

A play has a **setting.** Where does this play take place?

Many things happen to Mouse in this play. First Storyteller tells about Mouse and his boat. Who speaks next? Who answers? What does West Wind do to Mouse?

## Practice

**A.** Write answers to these questions.

1. How many different characters are in this play?
2. List three of the characters from this play.
3. Which character says, "What's going on?"
4. What are people who act out parts in a play called?
5. What is the <u>setting</u> of a play?

## Apply

**B. 6.** Write down some other things that could happen to Mouse. You and your class can plan a play. Mouse will be one character. Write the play with your class.

## A BOOK TO READ

Title: **The Stonecutter**
Author: Gerald McDermott
Publisher: Viking Press

"I wish to be the most powerful thing in the world." With this wish, awful things happened to Tasaku. He wanted to be rich like the prince. He wished for riches—and he got them! In time Tasaku became greedy. Read the book to find out some of the awful things that happened.

# 6 UNIT TEST

● **Describing Words**    pages 156–161

Write the letter of the describing word.

**1.** <u>Jo</u> <u>has</u> a <u>red</u> car.
   a  b    c

**2.** I <u>have</u> <u>four</u> <u>trucks</u>.
       a    b    c

**3.** <u>Ken</u> <u>seems</u> very <u>sad</u>.
   a    b      c

**4.** <u>You</u> use a <u>big</u> <u>toy</u>.
   a       b  c

● **Comparing Things**    pages 162–163

Choose the correct word. Write the sentences.

**5.** This oak tree is (tall, taller) than I am.
**6.** The maple is the (shorter, shortest) tree in my yard.

● **Maps**    page 170

Look at the map. Answer the questions.

**1.** On what street does Peter live?
**2.** Does a river cross Mill Road?

● **Note Taking**   page 171

Copy the rules you must follow when you take notes.

   **3.** Write notes in your own words.
   **4.** Copy each sentence you read.
   **5.** Tell only the important facts.

● **Sentence Combining**   page 172

Combine these sentences. Use the word <u>and</u>.

   **1.** Kittens scratch.   Kittens purr.

● **How-to Paragraph**   page 173

   **2.** Write this paragraph in the correct order.

      Brushing your teeth is easy. Next squeeze
   toothpaste on the brush. Last brush your front
   and back teeth. First get your toothbrush.

● **Writing and Editing a Book Report**   pages 174–177

   **3.** Think of a book you like. Write a book report on
   that book. Edit your report. Check to see that you
   used capital letters correctly.

● **Reading a Play**   pages 178–181

Choose the correct word in ( ). Write the sentences.

   **1.** People who act out a play are called (readers,
   actors).
   **2.** The (characters, setting) of a play is where the
   play takes place.
   **3.** The (characters, setting) in a play could be
   people or animals.

# MAINTENANCE and REVIEW

## Directions page 5

Write the number of the one sentence that is not a rule for following directions.

1. If you don't understand something, ask questions.
2. Talk softly to a classmate.
3. Listen carefully.
4. Say the directions to yourself.

## Parts of a Sentence page 28

Match these sentence parts. Write complete sentences.

5. The brown dog    have red and gold leaves.
6. Five small fish    barked all night.
7. The trees    swam in the bowl.

## Nouns pages 54–57

Find two nouns in each sentence. Write them.

8. My brothers traveled on a train.
9. Mother waved from the station.
10. A woman opened a window for them.
11. The boys visited Mr. Taylor.
12. The family lives in a tiny house.

## Verbs pages 86–87

13.–17. Look at sentences 8–12. Write the verb from each sentence.

## Paragraphs and Main Idea     pages 120–125

Copy the paragraph. Leave out the sentence that does not belong. Underline the sentence that tells the main idea.

18.     I learn many things in art class. I learn how to mix colors. My teacher shows me how to work with clay. Music class is interesting.

## Describing Words     pages 156–157

Write the word that describes each underlined noun.

19. I had hot <u>cereal</u> for breakfast today.
20. My red <u>bowl</u> was filled to the top.
21. I added many <u>raisins</u>.
22. I ate the cereal in five <u>minutes</u>.

## Words That Describe Feelings     pages 158–159

Write the words that describe feelings.

23. Manuel is angry at me today.
24. My teacher is happy with my work.
25. Jenny was surprised when she saw me.

## Comparisons     pages 162–163

Choose the correct word in ( ). Write the sentences.

26. Mr. Lopez is (taller, tallest) than Jimmy.
27. Bobby is the (taller, tallest) boy in his class.
28. Only the teacher is (taller, tallest) than he is.

# REVIEW HANDBOOK

GRAMMAR

## Sentences

sentence
- A **sentence** is a group of words that tells a complete thought. Every sentence begins with a capital letter.   page 26

  The balloon is red.

statement
- A **statement** tells something. It ends with a period (.).   page 29

  Pablo walked to the store.

question
- A **question** asks something. It ends with a question mark (**?**).   page 30

  Is that shirt new?


## *Practice*

A. Write only the groups of words that are sentences.

1. inside a big box
2. The bus is yellow.
3. two small dogs
4. Ed has a new bike.

B. Read the sentences. Write <u>statement</u> for a telling sentence. Write <u>question</u> for an asking sentence.

5. Is Jenny tired?
6. The water is cold.
7. My cat ran away.
8. What is your name?

# Nouns

- A **noun** is a word that names a person,    **noun**
  place, or thing.    page 56

    sister    farm    car

- Add **s** to most nouns to mean more than
  one.    page 62

    frog — frogs        boy — boys
    school — schools    tree — trees

- Add **es** to most nouns that end in **x, ch, sh,**
  or **s** to mean more than one.    page 62

    box — boxes      bench — benches
    dish — dishes    glass — glasses

## *Practice*

**A.** Copy the sentences. Underline the nouns.

1. Where is your brother?    2. The bus is empty.
3. The car is new.          4. A dog is barking.
5. Mother likes to read.    6. Is the school closed?

**B.** Write each noun. Then write the noun to mean
more than one.

7. window      8. pencil
9. dress      10. fox
11. ranch     12. train

# Verbs

action verb

- An **action verb** is a word that shows an action. page 86

  write   eat   build   talk

- Add **s** to an action verb that tells about one person or thing. page 88

  One cat <u>climbs</u>.   Three cats <u>climb</u>.

- Verbs can tell about action in the past. Form the past time of most verbs by adding **ed.** page 90

  Today I <u>paint</u>.   Yesterday I <u>painted</u>.

be, have

- Some verbs do not show action. page 92

  | **Present** | **Past** |
  |---|---|
  | am, is, are | was, were |
  | have, has | had |

## *Practice*

**A.** Copy the sentences. Underline the action verb in each sentence.

1. Wyatt walks home.
2. The turtle swims.
3. Father rakes leaves.
4. Nina sings **songs**.

**B.** Read each sentence. Write the verb. Write <u>now</u> or <u>past</u> after each verb.

5. Jill runs fast.
6. I talked to them.
7. Linda had a cold.
8. They are surprised.

# Go, Come, Run

- Some action verbs do not add **ed** to tell about the past.    page 98

irregular verbs

| Present | Past |
|---------|------|
| go(es) | went |
| come(s) | came |
| run(s) | ran |

## *Practice*

**A.** Write each sentence. Underline the verb. Write <u>now</u> or <u>past</u> after each one.

1. Otis goes to school.
2. I went to Ohio.
3. The deer ran away.
4. She came home.
5. We come with her.
6. They run fast.

**B.** Change each underlined verb. Make them tell about the <u>past</u>. Write the sentences.

7. My cat <u>runs</u> quickly.
8. Chet <u>comes</u> here after school.
9. Ann <u>goes</u> shopping.

**C.** Change the underlined verb. Make each sentence tell about <u>now</u>. Write the sentences.

10. Larry <u>came</u> home for lunch.
11. My friend <u>ran</u> in the race.
12. A turtle <u>went</u> into its shell.

# Describing Words

**describing
word**

- A **describing word** is a word that describes
a noun.     page 156

  I picked the <u>brown</u> puppy.

- Add <u>er</u> to most describing words when they are
used to compare two things.     page 162

  A horse is <u>taller</u> than a dog.

- Add <u>est</u> to most describing words when they are
used to compare more than two things.     page 162

  That is the <u>tallest</u> tree in the forest.

## *Practice*

**A.** Copy the sentences. Underline the describing
words.

1. The puppy is small.
2. A blue bike is outside.
3. Did you see the round ball?
4. My sister is happy.

**B.** Copy this chart. Fill in the describing words.

| | | |
|---|---|---|
| 5. high | higher | highest |
| 6. short | _____ | shortest |
| 7. _____ | taller | tallest |
| 8. fast | faster | _____ |

# Paragraphs

- A **paragraph** is a group of sentences that tell about one main idea.    page 120

  **paragraph**

- The first line of a paragraph is indented.
  page 120

## *Practice*

**A.** Copy each paragraph. Underline the sentence that tells the main idea.

1.  Last night I had a funny dream. I dreamt I won a prize. Guess what the prize was? I won 500 goldfish!

2.  Rachel and Jeremy like to roller-skate. They race each other. Jeremy skates backwards. Rachel skates at a rink.

**B.** Read each paragraph. Write the sentence that does not tell about the main idea.

3.  Tom planted a vegetable garden. He planted tomatoes. I like carrots and peas. Tom planted cucumbers and corn too.

4.  Maria likes the color yellow. She painted her bedroom yellow. Maria buys clothes and toys that are yellow. Bill has a green bike.

5.  Many people work in a school. The principal is in charge. Teachers teach children. Some schools have a nurse. Paul is sick today.

# Friendly Letters

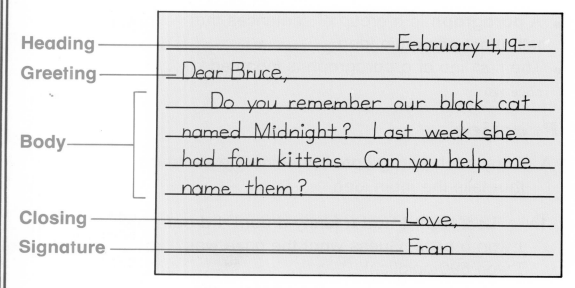

Heading — February 4, 19--

Greeting — Dear Bruce,

Body —
Do you remember our black cat named Midnight? Last week she had four kittens  Can you help me name them?

Closing — Love,

Signature — Fran

**letter**
- A **letter** has five parts: the heading, the greeting, the body, the closing, and the signature.  page 72
- Use a comma (,) between the day and the year in a heading.  page 72
- Use a comma (,) after the greeting and the closing.  page 72

## *Practice*

**A.** Copy the friendly letter above. The letter has five parts. Place the parts correctly on your paper. Use commas correctly.

**B.** Write a friendly letter to a relative. Tell what you do in school.

# Envelope

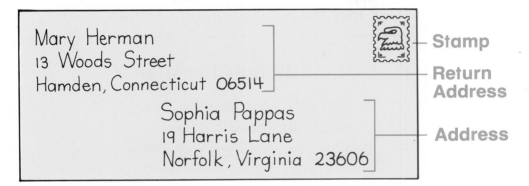

Mary Herman
13 Woods Street
Hamden, Connecticut 06514

     — Stamp

     — Return
       Address

    Sophia Pappas
    19 Harris Lane
    Norfolk, Virginia 23606

     — Address

- An **addressed envelope** has two parts.
  page 74
- The **address** tells who will receive the letter.   page 74
- The **return address** tells who is sending the letter.   page 74

**addressed envelope**

**address**

**return address**

## *Practice*

Draw a sample envelope on your paper.
Address the envelope correctly. Use this
address and return address.

To: Harold Greene
    113 White Street
    Palo Alto, California 94301

From: Nancy Benett
    80 Snow Road
    Merrill, Wisconsin 54452

# Editing

- Use this checklist when you edit your work.

### Editing Marks

≡ capitalize

⊙ make a period

∧ add something

⋏ add a comma

⌒ take something away

○ spell correctly

¶ indent the paragraph

## Editing Checklist

1. Did I tell a complete thought in each sentence?
2. Did I begin each sentence with a capital letter?
3. Did I end each statement with a period?
4. Did I end each question with a question mark?
5. Did I indent the first line of each paragraph?
6. Did I write a paragraph that has a main idea?
7. Did I write sentences that keep to the main idea of each paragraph?
8. Did I spell correctly?
9. Did I write neatly?

## *Practice*

Find a paragraph you wrote for science or social studies. Use the checklist to edit your work. Then write the paragraph correctly.

# Names and Titles of Persons and I

- Begin the name of a person with a capital letter.    page 58

    **person's names**

    Don Bracken    Maria Rodriquez

- Begin titles of people with capital letters. Put a period after <u>Ms.</u>, <u>Mrs.</u>, <u>Mr.</u>, and <u>Dr.</u>    page 58

    **titles of people**

- Always write the word <u>I</u> with a capital letter.    page 34

    **I**

# Names of Places

- Begin the names of streets with capital letters.    page 60

    **place names**

    61 Clinton Avenue

- Begin the names of cities and states with capital letters    page 60

    Houston, Texas    Portland, Maine

## *Practice*

**A.** Write the names correctly.

**1.** susie nolan    **2.** mr. alan wagner    **3.** ms. rosa rios

**B.** Write the sentences correctly.

**4.** Arnie lives on baker street in nome, alaska.
**5.** Does the train go to oregon and california?

# Names of Days, Months, and Holidays

**days** • Begin the name of a day of the week with a capital letter.  page 64

Monday    Wednesday    Saturday

**months** • Begin the name of a month with a capital letter.  page 64

March    June    September

**holidays** • Begin each important word in the name of a holiday with a capital letter.  page 64

Halloween    Fourth of July

# Names of Books and Stories

**titles** • Begin the first word, last word, and all important words in a title with a capital letter.  page 142

A Funny Surprise    The Cat in a Tree

## *Practice*

**A.** Write the words correctly.

| | |
|---|---|
| **1.** thursday | **2.** october |
| **3.** new year's day | **4.** sunday |
| **5.** july | **6.** independence day |

**B.** Write the titles correctly.

| | |
|---|---|
| **7.** the lost frog | **8.** harry and his neighbor |

# Punctuation

- Use a period (.) at the end of a statement. **period to end statements**
  page 29

    I have a pet hamster.

- Use a question mark (?) at the end of a question.    page 30 **question mark to end questions**

    Where are you going?

- Use an apostrophe (') to show that one or more letters have been left out in a contraction.    page 96 **apostrophe in contractions**

    was + not = wasn't

- Use a comma (,) between the name of a city and a state.    page 60 **comma in addresses**

    Mesa, Arizona    Lexington, Virginia

- Use a comma (,) between the day and the year in a date.    page 72 **comma in dates**

    September 8, 1954

## *Practice*

Write the sentences correctly. Use commas and apostrophes where needed. Add the correct mark to the end of each sentence.

1. We went to a fair
2. When did you go
3. It began July 3 1983
4. She hasnt gone

 **MORE PRACTICE**

# UNIT 1

### Listening and Speaking    pages 2–4

Write <u>Listening Rules</u> on your paper. Copy the rules
about listening. Then write <u>Speaking Rules</u>
on your paper. Copy the speaking rules.

1. Pay attention.
2. Say your words clearly.
3. Think about what to say.
4. Look at the person talking.
5. Speak so that everyone can hear you.

### Telephone Conversations and Introductions

pages 6–7

Read each sentence. Write the correct ways to
speak to others.

1. **a.** Hello. May I speak to Tony please?
   **b.** Let me speak to Tony.
2. **a.** Grandfather, this is Jean, my friend.
   **b.** Grandfather, here is Jean.

### ABC Order    pages 10–11

Write each group of letters in ABC order. The
letters will spell a word.

1. t o l        2. w o c        3. i d m

## ABC Order      pages 12–13

Write each list in ABC order.

1. trout      2. frog
   goldfish        snail
   shark          eel

## Writing Rhymes      pages 14–15

Finish the rhymes. Use the words in the box.

| spring    tree    out |
| --- |

1. From way up here I can see
   A pond and an apple _____.
2. My friends always shout
   For me to come _____.
3. In the tree robins sing,
   They are happy it is _____.

## Reading Poetry      pages 16–21

Copy the poem with rhyming words.

### Snail

Snail upon the wall,
Have you got at all
Anything to tell
About your shell?

           John Drinkwater

### Poem

I loved my friend.
He went away from me.
There's nothing more to say.
The poem ends,
Soft as it began—
I loved my friend.

           Langston Hughes

# UNIT 2

**Sentences**   pages 26–27

Write the word groups that are sentences.

1. very old clothes
2. We put on our coat.
3. Mother did not see us.
4. went to a store
5. The children are busy.
6. Paco fixed the wagon.

**Statements and Questions**   pages 29–31

Read each sentence. If the sentence is a statement, write <u>statement</u>. If the sentence is a question, write <u>question</u>.

1. Mandy has new mittens.
2. Where are the kittens?
3. My mother works in an office.
4. Does Scott have a new hat?
5. The shoes are brown.
6. Are your glasses lost?

**Word Order**   pages 32–33

Put the words in correct order. Write each sentence correctly.

1. to Alan went party a.
2. balloon got a He.
3. party The started noon at.
4. won children Some prizes.

## True and False Statements   page 38

Write <u>true</u> or <u>false</u> for each sentence.

1. Dogs can fly.
2. Lions can roar.
3. Snow is green.
4. Cats have soft fur.
5. Birds lay eggs.

## Writing and Editing Sentences   pages 40–43

Write two statements about yourself. Edit your sentences. Check to see that you used capital letters and periods correctly.

## Mechanics Practice   page 43

Write the sentences correctly.

1. some dogs help people
2. how do dogs learn
3. my dog is very smart
4. are some dogs helpful
5. do you have a dog
6. dogs make good pets
7. when did your dog have her puppies
8. how old are the puppies now

## Reading a Story   pages 44–47

Find a story in your reader. Read the story. Write three sentences about the story. Tell what happened <u>first</u>. Tell what happened <u>next</u>. Tell what happened <u>last</u>. Write the sentences on a piece of paper.

# UNIT 3

## Nouns   pages 54–57

Write the nouns in each group.

1. singer   eat   painter   dancer
2. read   clown   mother   friend
3. library   school   circus   sing
4. farm   town   bake   city
5. pencil   book   pen   sell
6. shoe   write   mitten   sock

## Names and Titles   pages 58–59

Write the names correctly.

1. wendy evans      2. mr burns
3. dr brown      4. mrs pilz
5. frank cuomo      6. miss rita sherman

## One or More Than One   pages 62–63

Make each noun name more than one. Write the nouns.

1. boy      2. class      3. bush      4. table
5. friend      6. watch      7. paper      8. glass

## Days of the Week, Months of the Year, and Holidays   pages 64–65

Write the days, months, and holidays correctly.

1. saturday      2. thanksgiving
3. april      4. new year's day

## Compound Words    pages 70–71

Make four compound words. Use a word from the box. Add it to a word with a number.

| | | | |
|---|---|---|---|
| bed | air | blue | pop |

**1.** bird    **2.** corn    **3.** room    **4.** plane

## Writing and Editing Letters    pages 72–79

Write an invitation. Use the letter parts below.

**1.** July 6, 19--    **2.** Dear Andy,
**3.** Your friend,    **4.** Please come to my house
**5.** (Your signature)    on Saturday. We can play
a new game.

## Mechanics Practice    page 79

Write these sentences correctly.

**1.** Does dr park live in wilmington delaware?
**2.** The last day of october is halloween.
**3.** mr ben fields and miss sue elks visited us.

## Reading Poetry    pages 80–81

Copy the poem. Underline the words that describe rain.

### Rain

Summer rain
is soft and cool,
so I go barefoot
in a pool.

Myra Cohn Livingston

# UNIT 4

### Verbs    pages 86–87

Copy the sentences. Underline the verb in each sentence.

1. Bud works in a flower shop.
2. I help my father.
3. We sell plants and flowers.
4. I talk to many people.
5. Ms. Lee buys daisies and tulips.

### Now or in the Past    pages 88–91

Read each sentence. Write <u>now</u> for each sentence that tells about now. Write <u>past</u> for each sentence that tells about the past.

1. Dr. Greene walks to work.
2. Mrs. Lipman called us last week.
3. Sarah cleaned the car.
4. Vernon fixed the wagon.
5. Billy works very hard.

### Forms of <u>Be</u> and <u>Have</u>    pages 92–95

Finish each sentence with a verb. Write the complete sentence.

1. I _____ hungry now.          is      am
2. Terry _____ a bad cold.       has     have
3. Brian _____ not here.         is      are
4. The flowers _____ in a box.   was     were
5. We _____ a pet dog.           have    has

## Dictionary Skills    pages 102–103

Read the entry. Write the correct answer in ( ).

> **cry** [krī] **1.** v. To weep or sob. **2.** To call out loudly or shout.

1. This entry lists (one, two) meanings for the word.
2. This entry should be on the same page as the guide words **(cake–choose, cow–cut).**

## Choosing Verbs and Editing Sentences
pages 106–109

Use interesting verbs in place of these verbs. Write each interesting verb in a sentence of your own. Then edit your sentences.

**1.** run    **2.** talked    **3.** looked    **4.** move

## Mechanics Practice    page 109

Use contractions in place of the underlined words. Write the sentences.

1. Taro <u>is not</u> here.
2. I <u>have not</u> eaten.
3. They <u>were not</u> hungry.
4. Holly <u>was not</u> coming.

## Reading a Story    pages 110–113

Finish the sentences.

1. The people in a story are called the _____.
2. The _____ is where a story takes place.
3. What happens in a story is called the _____.

# UNIT 5

## The Main Idea in Paragraphs    pages 120–123

Read each paragraph. Write the main idea.

1.    Laura and Ted work at an orange-drink stand. Many friends come to the stand. Ted pours the orange drink. Laura takes the money. They work hard.

   **a.** Laura and Ted's friends
   **b.** working at an orange-drink stand

2.    It is time for Laura and Ted to go home. Ted washes the pitcher. Laura folds the chairs. They both wash off the table.

   **a.** cleaning up the stand
   **b.** washing the pitcher

## Keeping to the Main Idea    pages 124–125

Read the paragraph. Write the sentence that does not tell about the main idea.

   Laura and Ted count the money they made. Laura puts the dimes in a pile. Ted sorts the other coins. Laura is very hungry.

## Antonyms    pages 128–129

Write the antonyms in each pair of sentences.

1. Chan looked up. Then he looked down.
2. Which way is right? Which way is wrong?
3. Should he go north? Should he go south?

## Words That Sound the Same   pages 130–131

Pick the correct word in ( ) to complete each sentence. Write the sentences.

1. Lee's home is by the (see, sea).
2. We walked on a dirt (road, rode).
3. Betty painted the fence (blew, blue).

## Prefixes and Suffixes   pages 132–135

Write the meaning for each word.

1. redo          2. hopeless
3. washable   4. unopened

## Writing and Editing a Story   pages 136–145

Were you ever lost? Write a story. Tell what you did or what you would do. Edit your story.

## Mechanics Practice   page 145

Write this paragraph correctly.

Earthworms are helpful. They build tunnels in soil. They loosen the soil so that plants can grow.

## Reading a Tale   pages 146–151

Write the answer to each question below.

1. What is a tale?
2. What are the people in a tale called?
3. What is the place where a tale happens called?

# UNIT 6

### Describing Words    pages 156–161

Copy the sentences. Circle the describing word in each sentence. Underline the noun it describes.

1. This popcorn tastes salty.
2. There are five wagons.
3. The baby is tired.
4. The loud noise scared Gordon.
5. Cotton feels soft.
6. We built a small birdhouse.

### Comparing Things    pages 162–163

Pick the correct word in ( ). Write the sentences.

1. My kitten is (small, smaller) than your dog.
2. The turtle is the (smaller, smallest) animal in the store.
3. The baby bird is (smallest, smaller) than a frog.
4. This parrot is (loud, louder) than yours.
5. This fish tank is the (cleaner, cleanest) one in the store.

### Using the Library    pages 166–167

Write <u>fiction</u> or <u>nonfiction</u> for each book title.

1. <u>Questions and Answers About Horses</u>
2. <u>The Wizard and His Magic Spells</u>
3. <u>The Witch's Vacation</u>
4. <u>Facts About Fish</u>

## Finding Information in a Book pages 168–169

Pick the correct word in ( ). Write the sentences.

1. The writer of a book is the (author, title).
2. The (index, title) is the name of the book.
3. The (table of contents, title) lists the chapters of a book.
4. The (index, author) is in ABC order.

## Combining Sentences page 172

Join these sentences. Use the word <u>and</u>.

1. Ray dressed. Ray ate breakfast.
2. Lily caught the ball. Lily threw it.

## Writing and Editing a Book Report pages 174–177

Think of a book you like. Write a book report on that book. Edit your report. Check to see that you used capital letters correctly.

## Mechanics Practice page 177

Write these book titles correctly.

1. six outdoor games     2. your senses

## Reading a Play pages 178–181

Write <u>true</u> or <u>false</u> for each sentence about a play.

1. A play can be about people or animals.
2. Actors are people who act out parts in a play.
3. A play does not have a setting.
4. A play is supposed to be read aloud.

# INDEX

Nouns, 54–67, 116, 184, 187, 202
    to name days, months, and holidays, 64–65, 67, 79, 82, 196, 202
    to name one or more than one, 62–63, 67, 82, 117, 187, 202
    to name people, 58–59, 66, 79, 82, 116, 195, 202
    to name special places, 60–61, 67, 79, 82, 195

One or more than one, 62–63, 67, 82, 117, 187, 202
Opposites. See Antonyms

Paragraphs, 120-27, 152, 191
    beginnings of, 122–123, 126
    how-to, 173, 183
    indenting, 120, 142, 144–145, 191
    writing, 145
People
    names and titles of, 58–59, 66, 79, 82, 116, 195, 202
    nouns for, 54–55, 66, 187
Period
    editing mark for, 42, 108, 194
    at the end of a sentence, 29, 43, 48, 186, 197
    after titles, 58, 79, 195
Places
    names of, 60–61, 67, 79, 82, 195
    nouns for, 56–57, 82, 187
Plays, 178–181, 183, 209
Plot, in stories, 112, 205
Poems
    "At the Library," 166
    "Brooms," 81
    "Feet," 86
    "The Fenceposts Wear Marshmallow Hats," 83
    "First Snow," 80
    "A Full Moon Comes Up," 19
    "Kite Days," 18
    "The Moon's the North Wind's Cooky," 19
    "Poem," 199
    "Rain," 203
    "The Robin," 16
    "Snail," 199
    "Spring Is When the Grass Turns Green and Glad," 18
    "Way Down South Where Bananas Grow," 23
    "Winter Moon," 19
    "World of Sound," 20
    "Zebra," 21
Poetry, 16–21, 23, 80–81, 199
Prefixes, 132–133, 153, 207

Question mark, 30, 43, 48, 186, 197

Questions, 30–31, 37, 186
    and statements, 37, 40–41, 48–49, 51, 116, 200

Review Handbook, 186–197
Rhymes, in poetry, 14–17, 23, 199
Run, forms of, 98–99, 101, 189

Sentences, 25–37, 48, 50, 186, 200–201
    combining, 76–77, 83, 172, 183, 209
    editing, 42–43, 49, 108–109, 115, 201, 205
    parts of, 28, 36, 51, 184
    word order in, 32–33, 37, 48, 200
    writing, 27, 29, 31, 33, 35, 37, 41, 43, 49, 201
Setting, 112, 115, 150, 180, 183, 205
Speaking
    rules for, 4, 8, 22, 198
    on the telephone, 6, 9, 22, 198
Statements, 29, 36, 186
    and questions, 37, 40–41, 48–49, 51, 116, 200
    true and false, 38, 49, 201
Stories
    editing, 144-145, 207
    true, 110-113, 115
    writing, 136–143, 153, 207
Stories to read, 49, 201
    "Emma," 44–47
    "Jumbo," 110–113
Suffixes, 134–135, 153, 207
Synonyms, 68–69, 82

Table of contents, using a, 168–169, 208
Tales, 146–151, 153, 207
Telephone book, 104–105, 115
Telephone conversations, 6, 9, 22, 198
Telling Sentences. See Statements
Thank you notes, 74–75, 83, 192
Title page, using a, 168–169
To Memorize, 15, 35, 59, 91, 133, 167
True and false statements, 38, 49, 201

Unit Tests, 22–23, 48–49, 82–83, 114–115, 152–153, 182–183

Verbs, 86–95, 98–101, 114–115, 117, 184, 188–189, 204–205. See also Be; Come; Go; Have; Run
    interesting, 106–107, 115, 205
    irregular, 92–95, 98–101, 115, 189
    past tense, 90–91, 100, 114, 117, 204
    present tense, 88–89, 100, 114, 117, 204

Words that sound the same, 130–131, 153, 207

B 3
C 4
D 5
E 6
F 7
G 8
H 9
I 0
J 1